D1143900

Our choice:

INTRODUCTION

Time for Food guides are designed to help you find interesting and enjoyable places to eat in the world's main tourist destinations. Each guide divides the destination into eight areas. Each area has a map, followed by a selection of the restaurants, cafés, bars, pubs and food markets in that area. The aim is to cover the whole spectrum of food establishments, from gourmet temples to humble cafés, plus good food shops or delicatessens where you can buy picnic ingredients or food to cook yourself.

If you are looking for a particular restaurant, regardless of its location, or a particular type of cuisine, you can turn to the Food Finder, starting on page 4. This lists all the establishments reviewed in this guide by name (in alphabetical order) and then by cuisine type.

PRICES

Unlike some guides, we have not wasted space telling you how bad a restaurant is – bad or poor-value restaurants simply do not make it into the guide. Many other guides ask restaurants to pay for their entries, or expect the restaurant to advertise in return for a listing. We do neither of these things: the restaurants and cafés featured here simply represent a selection of places that the authors have sampled and enjoyed.

If there is one consistent criterion for inclusion in the guide, it is good value. Good value does not, of course,

mean cheap necessarily. Food lovers know the difference between a restaurant where the high prices are fully justified by the quality of the ingredients and the excellence of the cooking and presentation of the food, and meretricious establishments where high prices are merely the result of pretentious attitudes.

Some of the restaurants featured here are undeniably expensive if you consume caviar and champagne, but even haute cuisine establishments offer set-price menus (especially at lunchtime) allowing budget diners to enjoy dishes created by top chefs and every bit as good as those on the regular menu. At the same time, some of the eating places listed here might not make it into more conventional food guides, because they are relatively humble cafés or takeaways. Some are deliberately oriented towards tourists, but there is nothing wrong in that: what some guides dismiss as 'tourist traps' may be deservedly popular for providing choice and good value.

FEEDBACK

You may or may not agree with the author's choice – in either case we would like to know about your experiences. Any feedback you give us and any recommendations you make will be followed up, so that you can look forward to seeing your restaurant suggestions in print in the next edition.

Feedback forms have been included at the back of the book and you can e-mail us with comments by writing to: *timeforfood@thomascook.com.* No food guide can keep pace with the changing restaurant scene, as chefs move on, establishments open or close, and menus, opening hours or credit card details change. Let us know what you like or do not like about the restaurants featured here. Tell us if you discover shops, pubs, cafés, bars, restaurants or markets that

you think should go in the guide. Let us know if you discover changes – say to telephone numbers or opening times.

Symbols used in this guide

VISA	Visa accepted
◉	Diners Club accepted
MasterCard	MasterCard accepted
⊀	Restaurant
⛾	Bar, café or pub
🛒	Shop, market or picnic site
✆	Telephone
◉	Transport
②	Numbered red circles relate to the maps at the start of the section

The price indications used in this guide have the following meanings:

€	budget level
€€	typical/average for the destination
€€€	up-market

FOOD FINDER

Ancient Rome and Testaccio

This most visited area of Rome is also the one where you tend to find overpriced, touristy restaurants; however, there are several exceptions. Testaccio was the river port of Ancient Rome and today is the best place to sample the most traditional of Roman specialities.

ANCIENT ROME AND TESTACCIO
Restaurants

Agata e Romeo ❶

V. Carlo Alberto, 45

Ø 06 446 5842/
06 446 6115

◉ Metro A to Vittorio Emanuele

Open: Mon–Sat 1300–1430, 2000–2230, closed Sun

Reservations essential

All credit cards accepted

Creative Roman cuisine

€€€

Elegant restaurant where Agata skilfully prepares her own version of sophisticated Roman and southern Italian dishes using the best ingredients. Husband Romeo manages the dining room impeccably. Fish lovers, carnivores and vegetarians are all catered for on a menu that changes frequently. Good cheese platter and excellent puddings: if you have left room, try the *millefoglie* oozing with almonds and cream.

Ai Tre Scalini da Rosanna e Matteo ❷

V. S S Quattro, 30

Ø 06 709 6309

◉ Metro B to Colosseo; bus 85 to V. di San Giovanni in Laterano

Open: 1300–1500, 1800–2400, closed Mon

Reservations essential

All credit cards accepted

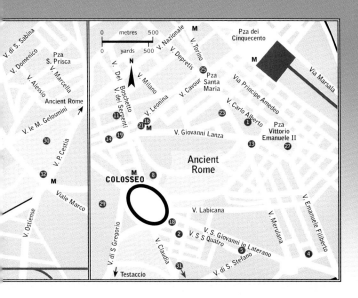

Classic cuisine

€€€

Two elegant, small dining rooms, one of which serves the modern, less hearty version of traditional Roman cuisine, whilst the other specialises in imaginative Italian and international dishes. Excellent game in season and a choice of vegetarian dishes. Deservedly sought after and just a stone's throw from the Colosseum.

Agustarello ❸

V. Giovanni Branca, 98–100

✆ 06 574 6585

🚌 Bus to V. Marmorata/V. Giovanni Branca

Open: 1230–1500, 1930–2300, closed Sun

Reservations recommended

No credit cards accepted

Traditional Roman cooking

€€

The sons of the late owner, Agustarello, carry on the tradition of reverently using every part of the animal including the thymus glands, pancreas and other unmentionable bits, but especially delicious when mixed with wild mushrooms. The trattoria's décor is very basic but there are outside tables where you can soak up the atmosphere of Testaccio. This place is very popular with locals and

the waiters' English varies between limited and non-existent.

Cannavota ❹

Pza San Giovanni in Laterano, 20

✆ 06 7720 5007

🚌 Bus 16, 85, 715 to V. Merulana

Open: 1230–1500, 1930–2300, closed Wed

Reservations recommended

All credit cards accepted

Roman trattoria

€€

Cheerful and bustling with an emphasis on traditional Roman dishes in generous portions. Good selection of risotto and pasta dishes with seafood: try the house speciality, *rigatoni alla cannavota* (pasta with a creamy tomato and seafood sauce).

Charly's Saucière ⑤

V. di San Giovanni in Laterano, 270

✆ 06 7049 5666

🚇 Bus 85 to V. di San Giovanni in Laterano

Open: 1300–1500, 2000–2400, closed Sun and lunch Sat and Mon

Reservations essential

All credit cards accepted

Franco-Swiss cuisine

€€€

Some say that this is the best of Rome's few French restaurants. Swiss influence shows in real fondues and *rosti*, together with featherlight soufflés and a superb choice of puddings. Good choice of wines with a definite French emphasis, complementing top-quality dishes.

Checchino dal 1887 ⑥

V. di Monte Testaccio 30

✆ 06 574 6318

🚇 Metro B to Piramide; bus to V. Marmorata or V. Galvani

Open: 1230–1500, 2000–2300, closed Sun evening and Mon

Reservations recommended

All credit cards accepted

Real Roman cooking

€€€

Amongst the trendy bars and clubs opposite the former slaughterhouse lies the foremost temple of authentic *cucina romana* (Roman food), which generally includes offal. The famous *coda alla vaccinara* (oxtail with tomato, pinenuts, raisins and bitter chocolate) was invented here. If offal is not for you, there is plenty more on the menu, including the delicious *abbacchio alla cacciatora* (baby lamb 'hunter style'). There is an excellent selection of cheeses and finest wines from the renowned wine cellar, which was dug out of the ancient amphora crocks and other broken pots which littered Monte Testaccio.

Da Felice ⑦

V. Mastro Giorgio, 29

✆ 06 574 6800

🚇 Metro B to Piramide; bus to V. Marmorata

Open: 1215–1430, 2000–2230, closed Sun

Reservations recommended

No credit cards accepted

Classic trattoria

€–€€

Good, traditional and plentiful Roman cuisine with specialities including tripe and *gnocchi* (dumplings) on appointed days. This is a very popular venue for big eaters and celebrities. Don't be put off by the lack of a sign on the door and the reserved notes on all the tables. If the owner likes the look of you, they are all miraculously removed. Well worth a visit as its ever-growing popularity shows.

Hostaria Nerone

V. Terme di Tito, 96	
✆ 06 474 5207	
Ⓜ Metro B to Colosseo	
Open: daily 1200–1500, 1900–2300	
Reservations recommended	
All credit cards accepted	
Roman trattoria	
€	

Views from the terrace over the Colosseum and the ruins of the Baths of Trajan make this a very touristy spot, but popular also with locals. However, a good *antipasti* buffet and steaming plates of pasta *alle vongole* and pasta *fagioli* are reliable fare in this well-managed family-run eatery, now also gaining a reputation as one of Rome's few gay restaurants.

Perilli ⑨

V. Marmorata, 39	
✆ 06 574 2415	
Ⓜ Metro B to Piramide	
Open: 1230–1500, 1930–2200, closed Wed	
Reservations recommended	
No credit cards accepted	
Traditional Roman	
€ €	

▲ Owners of Checchino dal 1887

Established over a century ago, this restaurant is always packed with hungry regulars tucking into robust, rustic traditional fare. Classic Roman dishes of *carciofi alla romana* (whole Roman artichokes), spaghetti *alla carbonara* and tasty tripe and lamb's offal contrast with vegetarian offerings. Wine is served by the carafe in a lively, convivial atmosphere, although the murals are not to everyone's taste.

Tuttifrutti ⑩

V. Luca della Robbia, 5	
✆ 06 575 7902	
Ⓜ Bus to V. Marmorata/V. Galvani	

Open: 2000–2400, closed Mon	
Reservations recommended	
𝖵𝖨𝖲𝖠 ⬤	
Modern Italian	
€	

Unprepossessing décor in a Testaccio side street is more than compensated by the inventive cuisine, with some international touches based on seasonal ingredients. The young, enthusiastic waiters talk you through the menu which changes nightly and the kitchen stays open late.

ANCIENT ROME AND TESTACCIO
Bars, cafés and pubs

Antico Caffè del Brasile ⑪

V. dei Serpenti, 23

🚌 Bus to V. Nazionale

Open: Mon–Sat 0645–2030

Traditional, characterful bar whose faithful following of distinguished customers has included the Pope when he lived in the area and was still only Cardinal Wojtyla. As you would expect from the name, the bar serves excellent coffee too.

Bar del Mattatolo ⑫

Pza Orazio Giustiniani, 3

🚌 Bus to V. Galvani/V. Marmorata

Open: daily 0600–2100

In the heart of Testaccio, this atmospheric little bar is especially busy first thing in the morning with revellers from near by clubland. In the old days it was the drinking spot for the slaughterhouse workers from across the road.

Bar e Altro di Gino Ponzi ⑬

V. dello Statuto, 48

🚇 Metro A to Vittorio Emanuele

Open: early every day until 2200

Newly opened bar and café in an area which has a shortage. Pasta *pomodoro basilico* (pasta with tomatoes and fresh basil) and 100 different kinds of pizza *ripiena* (stuffed) are very reasonably priced. Functional, but welcoming.

Le Café du Parc ㉜

Pza di Porta San Paolo

🚇 Metro B to Piramide; bus or tram to Pza di Porta San Paolo

Open: 0500–0200, closed Sun

In the midst of the frenetic Roman traffic, busy it may be, but it is the best place from which to admire the Pyramid of Cestius. The speciality is ice cream and it is worth splashing out on the excellent *cremolato affogato* – a creamy kind of sorbet. Also serves sandwiches, pizza and all drinks.

Cavour 313 ⑭

V. Cavour, 313

🚇 Metro B to V. Cavour; bus to V. Cavour

Open: 1230–1430, 1930–0030, closed Sun lunch Oct–mid-June

Very popular *enoteca* (wine bar) near the

Forum with a serious selection of over 500 bottles in the cellar. Amongst the rich, dark mahogany décor and a very friendly ambience choose from a variety of reasonably priced hot and cold snacks as well as delicious cheese platters to complement your wine.

Chiosco Testaccio ⑮

V. Giovanni Branca (corner of V. Beniamino Franklin)

🚌 Bus to V. Marmorata or V. Zabaglia

Open: May–mid-Sept 1200–0130

Tangy lemon, tamarind and coconut ice creams are the kiosk's speciality. Something of an institution in Testaccio, its history goes back over 80 years, although nowadays the ice is cut mechanically.

Pizzeria Leonina ⑯

V. Leonina, 84

🚇 Metro B to V. Cavour; bus to V. Cavour

Open: Mon–Fri 0730–2200

This pizzeria is always busy, so be prepared to queue, but it is worth it for one of the best *pizza a taglio* (pizza by the slice) in Rome, with delicious savoury

▲ The Colosseum

toppings and even an apple strudel topping for the sweet-toothed.

L'Oasi della Birra ⑰

Pza Testaccio, 41

🚇 Bus to V. Marmorata

Open: daily 0730–0100, closed Sun in July and all of Aug

Beer, as opposed to wine drinking, is becoming increasingly popular with young Italians. This oasis in the basement of an *enoteca* has over 500 to choose from, including Belgian Trappist seriously potent beers. A good variety of snacks is on offer, as well as hearty main meals such as goulash. For non-beer drinkers, there's a good wine list.

Il Ristoro della Salute ⑱

Pza del Colosseo, 2A

🚇 Metro B to Colosseo

Open: daily 0800–0200

No credit cards accepted

This bar, *gelateria*, *pasticceria* and café benefits from stunning views just across the road from the Colosseum. It serves sandwiches, pizzas and excellent chocolate-studded ice cream *tartufo*. Very popular with those on the tourist trail – try to get a pavement table for a bird's-eye view of the ruin to beat all ruins.

Da Valentino ⑲

V. Cavour, 293

🚇 Metro B to V. Cavour; bus to V. Cavour

Open: Sat–Thu 1200–1500, 1900–2200

A tiny and unassuming old-fashioned Roman trattoria focusing mainly on traditional Roman cuisine with a good value set menu. Excellently placed for the Forum, this is a good spot for lunch and very popular with locals.

Volpetti Più ⑳

V. Alessandro Volta, 8/10

🚇 Bus to V. Marmorata

Open: Mon–Sat 1000–1530, 1700–2230

Salads, pasta, pizzas and salamis are served up café-style just around the corner from its parent, the delicatessen **Volpetti** (*see page 14*). It also serves a good range of wines at reasonable prices.

ANCIENT ROME AND TESTACCIO
Shops, markets and picnic sites

Shops

La Bottega del Cioccolato 21

V. Leonina 12/14

Metro B to V. Cavour; bus to V. Cavour

Open: 0930–1930, closed Sun

All credit cards accepted

Fifty different kinds of chocolate (white, milk, bitter and filled) made on the premises from Brazil's best cocoa beans make this into a chocoholic's paradise. Conveniently close to the Colosseum, it is also part of the family-run chocolatiers, **Moriondo** (see page 44).

Il Canestro 22

V. Lucca della Robbia, 12

Bus to V. Marmorata

Open: Tue–Sat 0900–2000, Mon 1200–2000

A natural health and organic foods store, including Italian regional specialities. It also has homeopathic medicines and cosmetics.

Cottini 23

V. Merulana, 287

Metro A to Vittorio Emanuele

Open: daily 0700–2100

This bar, *pasticceria* and *gelateria* serves especially mouth-watering cakes. Between 1200 and 1500 there is also a self-service café where you can get good pizza and pasta.

Giolotti a Testaccio 24

V. Amerigo Vespucci, 35

Bus to V. Marmorata/ Pza dell'Emporio

Open: 0700–1300, closed Wed

You will be spoilt for choice with every permutation of coffee and *gelato* here. A good option is to do as the Romans and combine the two in a delicious *granità di caffè* (coffee with ice). There are some pavement tables, which are much in demand in this popular, characterful Testaccio institution.

The Korean Market 25

V. Cavour, 84/86

Bus to V. Cavour or Pza Esquilino

Open: Mon–Sat 0900–1300, 1600–2000, Sun 1530–1830

Sumptuous Korean produce abounds in this up-market emporium: another sign of Rome's burgeoning immigrant population bringing over their deliciously exotic foodstuffs.

Volpetti 26

V. Marmorata, 47

Website: *www.volpetti.com*

Bus to V. Marmorata

Open: Mon–Sat 0800–1400, 1700–2000, closed Sun and Tue evening

This famous 100-year-old store in Testaccio has everything from handmade pasta to long ageing or fresh young cheeses, whole hams, the most virgin of olive and truffle oils and wines, including a delicious white wine to accompany cheese. The owners, Claudio and Emilio, are especially interested in products which are in danger of extinction and despatch their goods all over the world – just as well as you may be tempted to buy far more than you can carry back!

Markets

Piazza Vittorio Market 27

Pza Vittorio Emanuele II

Metro A to Vittorio Emanuele

Open: Mon–Sat 0630–1330, closed Sun

This is central Rome's biggest and most colourful general market. As well as the usual Italian produce, exotic spices and pulses, kosher and halal meat are on display. It is also a melting pot of Indian, Chinese, Korean and African flavours. Even if you do not go to buy, it is a great spot for photo opportunities.

Testaccio Market ㉘

Pza Testaccio

🚇 Metro B to Piramide;
bus 11, 27

Open: 0730–1330, closed Sun

Relaxed, covered market which takes up the centre of the piazza. The freshest of fruit and vegetables are at the heart, lined on the perimeter by grocers, fishmongers and butchers. Excellent quality produce is available at extremely reasonable prices – very popular with the local residents.

Picnic sites

Palatine Hill ㉙

🚇 Metro B to Colosseo

Here, on the first of Rome's seven hills to be inhabited, is the city's legendary birthplace. The views over the Colosseum and the Forum are superb and the cooler air extremely refreshing.

Testaccio Park, Monte Testaccio ㉚

🚇 Metro B to Piramide

After visiting Testaccio market, or perhaps the up-market deli Volpetti, seek out a bench in the park to enjoy your picnic al fresco in this colourful, historic area of Rome.

Villa Celimontana Gardens ㉛

🚇 Metro B to Colosseo

Open: daily from 0700 until dusk

Little known to tourists, this idyllic park has shady pines, laurel and exotic trees and an obelisk brought back from Egypt, dedicated to Ramses II. At the centre is a lovely 16th-century mansion built for the Dukes of Mattei, now the seat of the Italian Geographical Society.

▲ Piazza Vittorio Market

Cucina romana

When in Rome ...

The Romans know a thing or two about the pleasures of life. To their credit, and our delight, there are few things more eternally pleasurable than lingering over a leisurely meal in a fountain-splashed piazza, in the shade of a vine-covered pergola, or in a bustling trattoria. Other capitals of the world may have embraced international cuisine almost to the extent of obliterating their own character, but when in Rome prepare yourself for gourmet, sometimes gourmand, delights deeply rooted in the voluptuous Italian character.

The rich flavours of this, the Lazio region, are redolent of herbs, virgin olive oil, ricotta cheese, lamb and pork, traditionally based on the diet of the frugal and the poor. The lavish feasts of Ancient Rome including such 'delicacies' as swans' hearts and nightingales' tongues were only the privilege of the wealthy few. There was a time when fish was considered unworthy to be served to guests, and gentlemen who liked to go fishing were viewed with great suspicion. Later, under the guidance of Antony and Cleopatra and the emperor Augustus, who were all passionate anglers, the Romans learnt to appreciate fish in all its forms. Nowadays, seafood restaurants are amongst the best in the city – highly sought after and often seriously expensive. **Quinzi e Gabrieli** (*see page 40*), **Alberto Ciarla** (*see page 68*) and **La Rosetta** (*see page 40*) are at the top of their league. More fishy delights await at **Cantina Cantarini** (*see page 48*) – a lovely, vibrant trattoria specialising in fresh fish from Thursday to Saturday. In the heart of the *centro stórico*, **San Teodoro** (*V. dei Fienili, 49/51; Ø 06 678 0933; ⊙ bus to V. del Teatro di Marcello; open: lunch and dinner,*

▲ *Coda alla vaccinara*

closed Sun; all credit cards accepted; ❷❸), which has amongst its specialities *tonnarelli San Teodoro* (pasta with king prawns, tomatoes and courgettes), is also good value, especially in its setting amongst the medieval houses in the shadow of the Forum.

But the traditional *cucina romana* offal has its origins in Testaccio near the old slaughterhouse where many locals once worked. These butchers (*vaccinari*) were paid partly in cash and partly in discarded meat or the fifth quarter (*quinto quarto*) – intestines, brain, heart, liver – and other unmentionable bits of the beast. So evolved low-cost, high protein dishes such as *coda alla vaccinara* (braised oxtail with celery), *trippa alla romana* (tripe) and *rigatoni alla pajata* (pasta with milk-fed veal intestines). **Checchino dal 1887** (*see page 10*) invented many of these recipes and justifiably remains one of the city's top restaurants. The biggest concentration of eateries devoted to *cucina romana* are in the Testaccio area (*see* **Agustarello** *page 9*) but amongst the exceptions is **Betto e Mery** (*V. dei Savorgnan, 99; ✆ 06 2430 5339;* Ⓜ *metro A to Arco di Travertino; open: evenings only, closed Thu; no credit cards accepted;* ❸) which is out of the centre, but worth the journey for a delicious offal experience.

The lavish feasts of Ancient Rome including such 'delicacies' such as swans' hearts and nightingales' tongues were only the privilege of the wealthy few.

Another variation of *cucina romana* is Jewish cuisine with its plump tender Roman artichokes, *carciofi alla romana* (in oil and garlic) and *carciofi alla giudia*, deliciously peppery and crisp fried in oil. To enjoy these at their best, visit the famous restaurant **Piperno** (*see page 31*) in the Jewish Ghetto. A less expensive but excellent option in the heart of the ghetto is **Da Giggetto** (*see page 30*) where the *fillets of baccalà* (cod) are superb.

Yet even with all these robust dishes, vegetarians are well catered for in the city: pasta, risotto, wonderful fresh vegetables and famous Roman *bruschetta*, 'lightly burnt bread' in Roman dialect, with countless delicious toppings, are to be found almost everywhere. **Margutta Vegetariano** (*see page 60*) is the original vegetarian restaurant on exclusive, arty Via Margutta. Worth trying also are **Arancia Blu** (*V. dei Latini, 65; ✆ 06 445 4105;* Ⓜ *bus to Porta Tiburtina; open: lunch and dinner daily; no credit cards accepted;* ❷❸), which serves excellent pasta dishes, macrobiotic food and a good range of wines, and **L'Insalata Ricca** (*Largo dei Chiavari, 85; ✆ 06 6880 3656;* Ⓜ *bus to Corso V. Emanuele; open: lunch and dinner daily; all credit cards accepted;* ❸). This is a particularly good salad bar which also serves pasta.

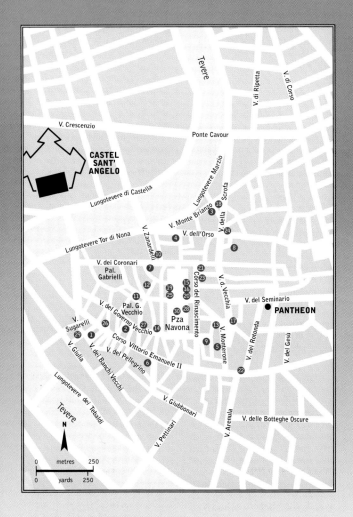

Around Piazza Navona

At the heart of the historic centre of Rome, this labyrinth of medieval lanes around the city's most famous piazza has some excellent restaurants. As well as the established masters, new generations of chefs are emerging who are earning great praise.

AROUND PIAZZA NAVONA
Restaurants

Albistrò

V. dei Banchi Vecchi, 140A

✆ 06 686 5274

🚌 Bus to Corso Vittorio Emanuele II

Open: Thu–Tue 1230–1500, 1930–2300, closed Wed and Sun lunch

Reservations unnecessary

All credit cards accepted

International

€€

Seasonal dishes are the speciality at this bistro-style restaurant where the tables spill out into a pretty courtyard in the heart of the *centro stórico*. The Swiss owner and his Italian wife are creative in their cuisine which is devoted to seasonal ingredients. Good wine list at reasonable prices.

Da Baffetto ❷

V. del Governo Vecchio, 114

✆ 06 686 1617

🚌 Bus to Corso Vittorio Emanuele II

Open: daily 1830–0100, closed lunch and two weeks of Aug

Reservations not allowed

No credit cards accepted

Pizzeria

€

This hole-in-the-wall pizzeria in the *centro stórico* is an institution, serving arguably the best pizzas in the city.

Be prepared to queue as it is crowded every evening with locals and tourists, so come early or late – orders are taken after midnight – but it really is well worth the wait.

La Campana ❸

Vicolo della Campana, 18

✆ 06 686 7820

🚇 Metro A to Spagna,

Open: 1230–1500, 1930–2330, closed Mon

Reservations recommended

All credit cards accepted

Roman cuisine

€€

Established in the 16th century, this trattoria claims to be Rome's oldest and, judging by its regular, well-heeled clientele, one of its most popular too. Traditional fare, including good *antipasti*, sumptuous pastas, hearty meat dishes and grilled fish are served in comfortable and very welcoming surroundings.

Il Convivio ❹

Vicolo dei Soldati, 31/V. dell'Orso, 44

✆ 06 686 9432

🚌 Bus to Corso del Rinascimento

Open: 1300–1430, 2000–2230, closed Sun and Mon lunch

Reservations essential

All credit cards accepted

Creative cuisine

€€€

Tiny, intimate restaurant, serving an imaginative mixture of flavours and textures: try *filletti di baccalà* (salted cod in batter) with gooseberry sauce. Although sometimes 'over creative', the menu is generally sophisticated with much emphasis on seasonal specialities.

L'Eau Vive ❺

V. Monterone, 85

✆ 06 6880 1095

🚇 Metro A to Barberini

Open: 1230–1430, 2000–2230, closed Sun (and 1–20 Aug)

Reservations recommended

🚍 💳 American Express

No smoking area upstairs

International-French

€€

Dine under vaulted ceilings in a 17th-century former palace, run by French missionary nuns. A modest set price menu is offered alongside couscous or classic fillet of beef flambéed with cognac, with an excellent selection of mainly French wines. This place was a favourite of Pope John Paul II's when he was archbishop of Krakow, and is now very popular with both secular and non-secular diners. Soothing and serene atmosphere – don't be surprised to hear the odd hymn!

Grappolo d'Oro

Pza della Cancelleria, 80

Ø 06 689 7080

🔘 Metro A to Spagna

Open: 1200–1500, 1915–0100, closed Sun

Reservations recommended

All credit cards accepted

Roman cooking

🄬🄲

Traditional trattoria very popular with tourists and locals, where owner Carlo Maggi gives a warm and courteous welcome. Two panelled dining rooms play host to good Roman food where favourites such as *penne all'amatriciana* (pasta

with bacon and tomato) and hearty *trippa alla romana* (tripe with tomato and mint) are justifiably popular.

Montevecchio ⓻

Pza Montevecchio, 22

Ø 06 686 1319

🔘 Metro A to Spagna

Open: Tue–Sat 1930–2400

Reservations recommended

All credit cards accepted

Roman-Italian

🄬🄲

An atmospheric restaurant with lofty ceilings in an equally atmospheric area where Raphael had his studios and the infamous Lucrezia Borgia wove her intrigues.
Traditional recipes difficult to find elsewhere feature regional cooking as well as seasonal dishes. The strudel of *porcini* mushrooms is delicious, as are the pasta dishes and Sardinian specialities.

Myosotis ⓼

Vicolo della Vaccarella , 3/5

Ø 06 686 5554

🔘 Bus to Corso del Rinascimento

Open: 1230–1530, 1930–2330, closed Sun

Reservations recommended

All credit cards accepted

Creative and Roman cuisine

🄬🄲

▲ Fish at Myosotis

This family-owned restaurant serves superb food at reasonable prices in a very friendly atmosphere. There is a commitment here to the belief that using the best raw materials is the essence of great cooking. Fresh seafood every day, combined with fresh, rolled to order pasta or a choice of meats, including delicious fillet of pork with pecorino (sheep's cheese) sauce, are all complemented by a good selection of wines at honest, near *enoteca* prices. The name, Myosotis, is Latin for forget-me-not – once experienced never forgotten!

Papà Giovanni 9

V. dei Sediari, 4

✆ 06 686 5308

✪ Bus to Corso del Rinascimento (70, 87)

Open: 1300–1500, 2000–2300, closed Sun

Reservations recommended

All credit cards accepted

Creative and Roman cuisine

€€€

This ancient taverna, whose walls are lined with wine bottles, pays homage to its rustic origins with new and creative versions of the trattoria menu. Famous for its imaginative nouvelle cuisine, old Roman dishes have gradually been supplanted by new, sometimes exciting, inventions. Always busy – as is the wine list, featuring offerings from the superb cellar of Giovanni's son, Renato Sentuti. There is also a good list of olive oils.

Ristorante Passetto dal 1860 10

V. Zanardelli, 14/Pza San Apollinaire, 40

✆ 06 6880 3696

✪ Bus to Corso Rinascimento

Open: daily 1200–1500, 1900–2400

Reservations recommended

All credit cards accepted

Italian-Roman cuisine

€€–€€€

The Fioravanti brothers run this high-ceilinged, traditional restaurant just off the Piazza Navona. Oysters, truffles and caviar appear alongside *ossobuco*, *saltimbocca alla romana* and fresh fish. An extensive wine list featuring selections from all over the world adds to its popularity, especially with the locals.

Bar del Fico ⑪

Pza del Fico, 26/28

🚌 Bus to Corso Vittorio
Emanuele II (62, 64)

Open: Mon–Sat 0800–0200,
Sun 1300–0200

The piazza takes its
name from a frail fig
tree, located just off the
Piazza Navona, around
the corner from Bar
della Pace. A drink or
delicious homemade
cake here at a pave-
ment table is just the
excuse needed for
people watching – from
artists to politicians,
celebrities, posers and
tourists.

Bar della Pace (Antico Caffè della Pace) ⑫

V. della Pace, 3/7

🚌 Bus to Corso del
Rinascimento

Open: daily 0900–0200

Although called the
Antico Caffè, it's always
known as the Bar della
Pace where all the
beautiful 'happening'
people congregate at
night. By day it is
quieter – a good spot to
sit outside on the
wicker chairs or to sit
at a marble table and
enjoy the atmospheric
mahogany and mirrored
19th-century interior.
This is *the* place to see
and be seen.

La Crêperie di San Eustachio ⑬

Pza San Eustachio, 50

🚌 Bus to Corso del
Rinascimento

Open: Tue–Sun 1800–0200,
Sat–Sun 1230–0200

This very atmospheric
café-cum-wine bar and
crêperie is especially
popular with the young
crowd. Try the *roman-
tico – prosciutto crudo,
mozzarella e funghi*
(ham, mozzarella cheese
and mushrooms) or, for
the sweet-toothed, a
mouth-watering nutella
and chocolate crêpe.

Cul de Sac ⑭

Pza Pasquino, 73

🚌 Bus to Corso Vittorio
Emanuele II

Open: 1230–1530,
1900–0030, closed Mon
lunch

Choose from over 1 400
wines in Rome's original
wine bar, founded in
1968. An ample selec-
tion of mainly cold food
accompanies the reason-
ably priced liquid
refreshment and all
within a stone's throw
of Piazza Navona.

Dolce Vita ⑮

Pza Navona, 70A

🚌 Bus to Corso del
Rinascimento

Open: daily 0730–0200

Another perfect spot for
watching the world go
by from a table right on
the piazza, this much
photographed café-bar
also serves drinks and

▲ Bar della Pace

snacks. If you want to escape the crowds, there are a few tables inside. As you would expect from the location, fare doesn't come cheap.

Enoteca La Bevitoria 16

Pza Navona, 72

🚍 Bus to Corso del Rinascimento

Open: daily 0730–0200

Right on the piazza, next to Dolce Vita, this wine bar offers full restaurant service as well as *mescita* (wine-tasting by the glass with snacks), the better option. Not especially cheap, but the atmosphere and view more than compensate.

Sant'Eustachio 17

Pza Sant'Eustachio, 82

🚍 Bus to Corso del Rinascimento

Open: daily 0830–0100

Reputedly serves the best coffee in Rome and is certainly the city's most famous coffee bar. Queue at the till for your caffeine fix, the speciality is the deliciously frothy *gran caffè* (sweet, black and strong) and remember that you can send extra supplies home – or all over the world.

Tartarughino 18

V. della Scrofa, 1

🚍 Bus to V. di Ripetta (70, 87)

Open: 2100–0400, closed Sun

▲ Sant'Eustachio

A piano bar popular with the over-forties, conservative it may be, but its popularity over the last 20 years shows no sign of waning. Elegant venue patronised by lots of financial and political movers and shakers.

Tre Scalini 19

Pza Navona, 28/32

Tel: 06 687 9148

🚍 Bus to Corso del Rinascimento

Open: 0800–0100, closed Wed (and 7 Jan–19 Feb)

Rome's best known piazza's most famous bar serves the celebrated *tartufo* ice cream. Named after its resemblance to the shape of the exotic knobbly truffle, this divine chocolate-studded ice also has cherries and swirls of whipped cream – a meal in itself. But there's a full restaurant menu too with the usual specialities such as risotto *ai porcini* or *carpaccio* of sea bass. Perfect for celebrity spotting from a table on the piazza.

Tucci 20

Pza Navona, 94–100

🚍 Bus to Corso del Rinascimento

Open: 0900–2400, closed Mon (open daily in summer)

Right on the piazza, from here you have a bird's-eye view of Bernini's watery masterpieces. Not cheap, but serves good *gelati* as well as restaurant meals, snacks and drinks.

Shops

Ai Monasteri ㉑

Pza delle Cinque Lune,
76/Corso del Rinascimento,
72

🚌 Bus to Corso del
Rinascimento

Open: 0900–1300, 1630–
1930, closed Sun and Thu
am

No credit cards accepted

A distinct ecclesiastical
atmosphere pervades
this well-established
shop (founded in 1892)
selling products from
most of the monastic
orders throughout Italy.
Choose from the herby
amaro benedittino – a
liqueur discovered by
15th-century monks –
or grappas, originally
the 'poor man's liqueur',
to honey, preserves,
wines and other natural
products which will
make a holy hole in the
pocket. All of them are
delectable goods which
make excellent sou-
venirs. (Here you will
even find cosmetic prod-
ucts for dogs and cats!)

Antica Norcineria ㉔

V. della Scrofa, 100

🚌 Bus to Corso del
Rinascimento

Open: daily, closed Sat pm in
summer and Thu pm in
winter

As well as **Volpetti** (no
31), this is the place to
come to stock up on
picnic goodies and other
mouth-watering treats.

Brek ㉒

Largo Argentina, 1

🚌 Bus/tram to Largo
Argentina

Open: daily 0700–0100

Next door to the Teatro
Argentina, this very
theatrical bar serves
delicious slices of pizza
downstairs. Upstairs
there is a grill and
salad bar.

▲ Ai Monasteri

Cinque Lune 🟤23

Corso del Rinascimento, 89

🚌 Bus to Corso del Rinascimento

Open: 0800–2130, closed Mon

One of the best cake-shops in Rome – as well as one of the smallest. The fresh cream-filled varieties are especially delicious and the choux pastry has no equal in the city. It is also very good for celebratory cakes, including tantalising offerings at Christmas and Easter.

Il Domiziano e Caffè di Colombia 🟤25

Pza Navona, 88

🚌 Bus to Corso del Rinascimento

Open: 0900–0130, closed Thu

Buy a delicious creamy cake or gorgeous *gelato* at this popular, bustling *pasticceria*, *gelateria* and bar right on the Piazza Navona.

In Folio 🟤26

Corso Vittorio Emanuele II, 261/263

🚌 Bus to Corso Vittorio Emanuele II (62, 64)

Open: Tue–Sat 1000–2000, Mon 1530–2000, closed Sun

Cheerful, well lit shop featuring all kinds of gadgets and fun gizmos for the kitchen amongst other household designer goods. Look out especially for the latest in coffee-pots and beautifully shaped, transparent vases. As

well as the 21st century, the 1940s and 50s are well represented here too, where the accent is firmly on style.

Fratelli Paladini 🟤27

V. del Governo Vecchio, 29

🚌 Bus to Corso Vittorio Emanuele II

Open: Fri–Wed 0800–2000, Thu 0800–1500, closed Aug

Lovely old, family-run bakery specialising in wood-fired pizza *bianca* which you can have filled to order with any number of tasty combinations. It can get very busy at peak hours of the day.

De Sanctis 🟤28

Pza Navona, 82/84

🚌 Bus to Corso del Rinascimento

Open: 1000–1300, 1600–2000, closed Sun and Mon am

The place to come for inspiration on tableware. Here you will find an excellent selection of Alessi products designed by Alberto Alessi, who has developed his kitchen and tableware business into the cutting edge of contemporary design. Everything from ceramics to coffee-pots, dinner services, saucepans and original stainless steel objects are all displayed with works by other designers.

Stock Market 🟤29

V. dei Banchi Vecchi, 51/52

🚌 Bus to Corso Vittorio Emanuele II

Open: 1000–1300, 1600–2000, closed Sun–Mon

Cheap but classy kitchen implements and crockery – everything for the home and much more besides.

M & M Volpetti 🟤24

V. della Scrofa, 31

🚌 Bus to Corso del Rinascimento

Open: daily

Gourmet snacks at higher than average prices at this up-market *rosticceria*/sandwich bar, which is always very busy because of the high quality of the food. Expect to queue around lunchtime.

Picnic sites

Piazza Navona 🟤30

🚌 Bus to Corso del Rinascimento

Nowhere more than in the Piazza Navona is the stage-set of Rome more striking. A picnic by Bernini's *Fountain of the Four Rivers* will ensure that you have a part in the river of life as others perch on the steps, gesticulate wildly and everyone and anyone congregates to gossip, picnic, have an ice cream or just cool off on a marble bench next to the refreshing cascades. This is the hub of Rome's *centro stórico*.

Pizza and pasta

The joys of living?

In 1861, the year of the unification of Italy under the rule of the House of Savoy, the young Mrs Beeton, in her book, *Household Management*, wrote 'modern Romans are merged in the general name of Italians, who, with the exception of macaroni, have no specially characteristic article of food'. Pasta is still the mainstay of the Italian meal (not for nothing is it called '*il primo*'), but what a wealth of colours, varieties, textures and sheer numbers she missed! Conservatively estimated at 350 different shapes, all have gloriously poetic names: *farfalle (butterflies)*, *capelli d'angelo* (angel hair), *conchigliette* (small shells), *cappelletti* (little hats), *fettuccine* (tagliatelle), *fusilli* (corkscrew-shaped), *ziti* (bridegrooms) and tortellini (famously said to be inspired by the shape of Venus's navel).

La pasta è gioia di vivere – pasta is the joy of living – this is

the motto of the world's only museum devoted to pasta. In the unique **National Pasta Museum (Museo Nazionale delle Pasta Alimentari)** (*Pza Scanderberg, 117, nr Pza del Quirinale; ✆ 06 699 1119; open: daily 0930–1730*), 11 rooms tell the story of pasta and how this originally poor country has made a virtue out of necessity by creating a balanced way of eating using the most traditional of its crops, and why cooking it '*al dente*' (slightly resistant) makes it more easily digestible.

Spaghetti alla carbonara – made with *pancetta* (cured bacon), egg yolk and cheese is perhaps the best known of all Roman pasta dishes together with *spaghetti alle vongole* (with clams and tomatoes) – best on Tuesdays and Fridays when the clams are guaranteed to be really fresh. But *all'amatriciana* (with a sauce of tomato, chilli and *pancetta*) and *penne all'arrabbiata* (literally angry quills) with its fiery sauce of chilli and tomato, feature everywhere too. *Al cacio e pepe* is perhaps the simplest variation of all: pasta with grated fresh pecorino *romano* (tangy cheese made from ewes' milk), extra virgin olive oil and ground black pepper. This is especially fashionable in the *cucina povera* school – a new retro trend in up-market restaurants. Other favourites include *gnocchi alla romana*, delicious little dumplings made in the traditional Roman way with semolina flour and usually served with a tomato or meat *ragù* sauce – Thursday is *gnocchi* day in Rome.

The pizza, another Italian invention, shows no sign of losing its popularity and is a great snack or substantial meal at all times of the day and night – especially late for the locals. Most pizzerias are open only in the evenings and the huge variety ranges from the thick Napoletana version and *calzone* (folded-over) to pizza *romana*, thinner and crispier and, in its authentic version, made with onions and oil, no tomato. Always seek out places with wood ovens (*forno a legna*) – the results are so much better than from the electric version. In Trastevere, **Da Vittorio** (*see page 71*) claims to make the best pizzas in Rome.

... conservatively estimated at 350 different shapes, all have gloriously poetic names ...

Abruzzi ai S S Apostoli (*V. del Vaccaro, 1, Quirinale; ✆ 06 679 3897; open: lunch and dinner, closed Sat; reservations recommended; all credit cards accepted* ❶) has superb pasta *carbonara*. At Testaccio, **Remo** (*Pza Sta Maria Liberatrice, 44; ✆ 06 574 6270; 🚌 bus to V. Marmorata; open: evenings only, closed Sun;* ❶) is amongst the best for authentic pizza *romana*. **PizzaRé** (*V. di Ripetta, 14; ✆ 06 321 1468; 🚌 bus to Pza del Popolo; open: lunch and dinner daily;* ❶) serves 40 delicious varieties of Neapolitan pizza. **Panattoni**, better known as **L'Obitorio** (the mortuary) because

of its marble slab tables (*Vle Trastevere, 53; ✆ 06 580 0919; 🚌 bus to V. Trastevere; open: evenings, closed Wed; all credit cards accepted* ❶) is ironically a very lively pizzeria until very late. **Da Baffetto** (*see page 19*) most agree, is Rome's best and also busiest. If the queues at Baffetto are too off-putting, try its very good offshoot **La Montecarlo** (*V. dei Savelli, 12; ✆ 06 686 1877; open: daily; no credit cards accepted;* ❶). **Dar Poeta** (*Vicolo del Bologna, 45, on the corner of Pza della Scala; ✆ 06 588 0516; closed lunch and Mon;* VISA; ❶) has, as well as the savoury, delicious sweet variations too – try the apples and orange liqueur *la bodrilla*. **Acchiappafantasmi Pizzeria** (*V. dei Cappellari, 66; ✆ 06 687 3462; open: evenings only, closed Tue;* ❶), meaning 'ghostbusters', creates a Calabrian speciality – *pizza del campionato* – which even includes spooky looking olives for eyes. Good value and especially popular with the young set.

Around Campo de' Fiori

Everything from candlelit bistros to chic restaurants and lively trattorias cluster here in this very upwardly mobile area around the famous market. The ghetto is rich in atmosphere dating back over 400 years, and the restaurants reflect that tradition with cucina romana and Jewish dishes.

AROUND CAMPO DE' FIORI
Restaurants

Camponeschi ❶

Pza Farnese, 50

∅ 06 687 4927

🚌 Bus to Corso Vittorio Emanuele II

Open: 1930–0030, closed lunch and Sun

Reservations recommended

All credit cards accepted

Roman and seafood cuisine

€€€

Set in a beautiful square in the *centro stórico*, beside the French Embassy – originally the Palazzo Farnese – where Tosca killed the Chief of Police, this elegant restaurant serves slightly adapted Roman cuisine and very creative seafood, as well as international classics including game and soufflés. The décor shows off lovely restored vaults covered with frescos, all of which contributes to its popularity with celebrities and locals.

La Carbonara ❷

Pza Campo de' Fiori, 23 (north west side of market)

∅ 06 686 4783

🚌 Bus to Corso Vittorio Emanuele II

Open: 1215–1500, 1900–2330, closed Tue

Reservations recommended

All credit cards accepted

Roman cuisine

€€

As well as the house speciality, pasta *alla carbonara*, spaghetti *alle vongole* (with clams) has an enthusiastic following, as does *fritto di cervella e carciofi* (fried brains and artichokes) for the slightly more robust. Superbly

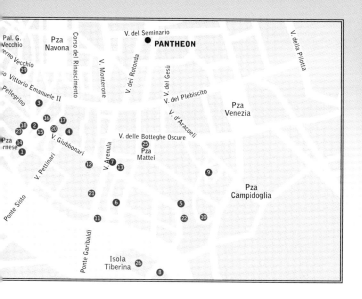

located right on the piazza, this old favourite manages to combine being a tourist trap with good, honest and not overpriced Roman food and wine.

Ditirambo ❸

Pza della Cancelleria, 74/75

✆ 06 687 1626

🚌 Bus to Corso Vittorio Emanuele II

Open: Tue–Sun 1300–1530, daily 2000–2330

Reservations recommended

💳

Creative modern Italian

€€

Very popular, friendly trattoria close to the Campo de' Fiori, which successfully combines

▲ Hand rolling pasta at Ditirambo

delicious homemade pasta with inspired vegetarian dishes, such as *maltagliati con i fiori di zucca* – pasta with courgette flowers – and classic Italian regional specialities including *bollito misto alla piemontese* (selection of boiled meats Piedmont style).

Filletti di Baccalà (officially Dar Filettaro a Santa Barbara) ④

Largo dei Librari, 88
✆ 06 686 4018
⬤ Bus to Largo Argentina
Open: 1750–2310, closed lunch and Sun
Reservations not allowed

No credit cards accepted
Fish and chips *alla romana*
❻

Salt cod fillets in batter is what the sign promises and delivers, with great success. Eat in on formica tables in very basic surroundings, but with the added bonus of being in a very pretty piazza, or take out. Extras include fried courgettes at almost give-away prices. Eternally and deservedly popular.

Da Giggetto ⑤

V. del Portico d'Ottavia, 21A
✆ 06 686 1105

⬤ Bus to V. Arenula
Open: 1230–1500, 1930–2300, closed Mon
Reservations recommended
All credit cards accepted
Roman Jewish cuisine
❻❻

In the heart of the Jewish ghetto, next door to the Theatre of Marcellus. The usual classic dishes of *carciofi alla giudia* (crispy fried artichokes) and *filletti di baccalà* (salted cod fillets) are delicious, or for the less squeamish, try the excellent *rigatoni con pajata* – pasta with calf's intestines with the mother's milk still inside. This bustling

▲ Piperno

trattoria is extremely popular with locals and tourists alike.

Piperno

Monte de'Cenci, 9

☏ 06 6880 6629

🚌 Bus to V. Arenula

Open: Tue–Sat 1215–1430, 2000–2300, Sun 1230–1500

Reservations essential

All credit cards accepted

Roman Jewish cuisine

●●●

Tucked away in a quiet, secluded square, this bastion of Roman Jewish cookery dates back to around 1860, founded by Pacifico Piperno, to whom Jewish cooking is much indebted. Conservative and expensive it is, but despite much competition, the crispy fried artichokes, *carciofi alla giudia*, are without equal, as are the succulent fried courgette (*zucchini*) flowers, tripe and superb fish. Excellent wine list.

Al Pompiere ⑦

V. Sta Maria de'Calderari, 38

☏ 06 686 8377

🚌 Bus to Pza Mattei

Open: 1200–1500, 1930–2300, closed Sun

Reservations unnecessary

●● ▨

Roman cuisine

●–●●

Dine under frescos and open-beamed ceilings in this huge dining room,

once a 16th-century palazzo. Even so, the ambience is homely rather than palatial and good, reasonably priced food includes classic Roman dishes and delicious ricotta and sour plum tart.

Sora Lella ⑧

V. Ponte Quattro Capi, 16, Isola Tiberina

☏ 06 686 1601

🚌 Bus to Pza Monte Savello

Open: 1300–1430, 2000–2300, closed Sun

Reservations recommended

All credit cards accepted

Roman cuisine

●●●

Authentic Roman trattoria on a magical little island in the Tiber, next to Trastevere. Named after the larger-than-life sister of the late film star Aldo Fabrizzi, her son, also Aldo, perpetuates his late mother's loving devotion to old Roman recipes and traditional, authentic food. The menu features a sublime *pollo con peperoni* and the *abbacchio* (lamb) ranks amongst the best in Rome. Expensive, but met with great enthusiasm by the many celebrities – and lesser mortals – who are great fans of the location as well as the food.

Taverna degli Amici ⑨

Pza Margana, 36

☏ 06 6992 0637

🚌 Bus to Pza Venezia

Open: 1230–1530, 1930–2400, closed Monday

Reservations recommended

All credit cards accepted

Roman-Italian cuisine

●●

In a superb setting in a little piazza at the heart of the ghetto area, the kitchen is honest and straightforward with emphasis on traditional Roman food, the freshest of seafood and excellent wild mushrooms in season with other vegetarian variations on offer. A manageable wine-list and outdoor tables complete the appeal of this friendly, well-patronised taverna.

Vecchia Roma ⑩

Pza di Campitelli, 18

☏ 06 686 4604

🚌 Bus to V. del teatro di Marcello

Open: 1300–1530, 2000–2300, closed Wed

Reservations recommended

All credit cards accepted

Classic cuisine

●●

Quietly located between the Campidoglio, ghetto and the 'tortoise fountain', this trattoria is well known for its fresh seafood, sea bass (*la spigola*) and good pastas and risottos. Lamb is also a speciality, as is the ubiquitous veal. The wine list is somewhat encyclopaedic.

AROUND CAMPO DE' FIORI
Bars, cafés and pubs

Alberto Pica ⓫

V. della Seggiola, 12

🚍 Bus to Largo
Argentina/tram to V.
Arenula

Open: Mon–Sat 0800–0200,
Sun 1600–0300

Popular bar and *tavola
calda*, but most famous
for its excellent ice
cream. Choose from
around 20 flavours,
amongst which the rice
specialities are espe-
cially delicious. The

cinnamon rice, *riso alla
cannella*, is definitely
worth a try.

Bernasconi ⓬

Largo di Torre Argentina,
15/Pza Carioli, 16

🚍 Tram to V. Arenula

Open: daily 0700–2030

One of the oldest and
best cake shops in the
city. Sample the superb
cornetti (croissants
Italian style) and *lieviti*
(breakfast yeast buns) or
choose from some of

the most delicious
cream cakes you will
ever taste. Although it's
small inside, all of
Rome seems to congre-
gate here on a Sunday.
Also a very popular bar
in the daytime.

La Bottega del
Vino da Anacleto
Bleve ⓭

V. Sta Maria del Pianto
9A/11/12

✆ 06 685 5970

🚍 Bus to Largo Argentina

▲ La Bottega del Vino

Open: Tue–Sat 1245–1500, 1600–2000, dinner Wed–Fri 2000–2200

A wine shop, bar and restaurant which boasts over 2 000 different wines where the owner Anacleto Bleve's speciality is advice and hospitality. A mouth-watering selection of cold cuts, salads, pastas and particularly excellent cheeses accompanies the carefully selected range of bottles. The restaurant is very popular with the locals who know the excellent quality of food, so you would be well advised to book in advance.

Caffè Farnese ⑭

V. dei Baullari, 106

⊚ Bus to Corso Vittorio Emanuele II

Open: daily 0700–0200

On a corner of Piazza Farnese, this *pasticceria/gelateria* is a great spot for people watching, especially on a Saturday morning when the Campo de' Fiori market is at its busiest. Good *cornetti* to complement your cappuccino.

Drunken Ship ⑮

Pza Campo de' Fiori, 20/21

⊚ Bus to Corso Vittorio Emanuele II

Open: Mon–Sat 1700–0200, Sun 1000–0200

Excellent location with tables on the piazza make this the place to see and be seen. Inside, the décor is all dark

wood with an unmistakable slight tilt to it, as you would expect from the bar's name. This hugely popular, American-style hostelry has become the meeting place of the young of all nationalities. Stylish with happy hour from 1700 to 2000 and DJs later in the evening.

Enoteca Vineria (also known as Da Georgio) ⑯

Campo de' Fiori, 15

⊚ Bus to Corso Vittorio Emanuele II

Open: Mon–Sat 0930–1500, 1700–0100

Excellent location right on the Campo, this authentic wine bar is very popular with locals by day and the seriously beautiful young things at night. The pavement tables are always crowded and prices by the glass for good wine are very reasonable. If you want to buy a bottle late, this is the place to come.

Jam ⑰

V. dei Chiavari, 4

⊚ Bus to Corso Vittorio Emanuele II

Open: daily

New and very popular bar and restaurant which serves good pasta dishes including nettle risotto and ravioli stuffed with goats' cheese.

Latteria del Gallo ⑱

Vicolo del Gallo, 4

⊚ Bus to Corso Vittorio Emanuele II

Open: Thu–Tue 0830–1400, 1700–2400

This bar-*latteria* (it also sells dairy products) between Piazza Farnese and Campo de' Fiori remains in a timewarp with its marble slab tables and clientele of Rome's colourful hippies and ex-pats. The brave new millennium seems to have passed unnoticed by this Roman institution!

Il Piccolo ⑲

V. del Governo Vecchio, 74/5

⊚ Bus to Corso Vittorio Emanuele II (62, 64)

Open: daily 1800–0200

A cosy wine bar near to Piazza Navona whose tables inside and out are always crowded. Good value and great for watching the intellectual, arty crowd.

Vineria Reggio ⑳

Campo de' Fiori, 15

⊚ Bus to Corso Vittorio Emanuele II

Open: Mon–Sat 0930–1400, 1800–0100 (0200 on Sat)

A good spot for *mescita* (wine and nibbles), especially at night when the pavements outside are crammed with every sector of Roman life – from bikers and ageing hippies to serious intellectuals and every variation in-between. By day, it is a peaceful retreat for a glass of wine and sandwich.

AROUND CAMPO DE' FIORI
Shops, markets and picnic sites

Shops

L'Albero del Pane ㉑

V. Sta Maria del Pianto, 19/20 (crossroads of V. Arenula)

🚌 Bus to V. Arenula

Open: all day, every day

Healthfoods, macrobiotics, breads, herbs, delicatessen goods and natural cosmetics are all invitingly displayed in this shop that smells so fresh that you can almost feel it doing you good.

Cisternino Cooperativa fra Produttore di Latte di Lazio ⑱

Vicolo del Gallo, 18/19

🚌 Bus to Corso Vittorio Emanuele II

The title may be a mouthful, but delicious cheeses are bound to tempt you at this dairy near Piazza Campo de' Fiori. Whether your choice is cows', sheep or buffalo cheese, they are all excellent.

Dolceroma ㉒

V. del Portico di Ottavia, 20B

🚌 Bus to Lungoevere Cenci

Open: Tue–Sat normal shopping hours

Real Viennese pastries and American-style chocolate-chip cookies tempt your taste buds. Not the place to come if you want Roman specialities, but they are all delicious and make a pleasant, if fairly expensive, change.

Il Forno del Ghetto ⑯

Pza Campo de' Fiori, 22/22A

🚌 Bus to Corso Vittorio Emanuele II/tram to V. Arenula

Open: Sun–Fri, closed Fri after sundown, Sat and Jewish holidays

Here you will find a dazzling array of breads and delicious pastries in this famous takeaway Jewish bakery that looks just like a hole-in-the-wall from outside. The ricotta cake with chocolate or sharp cherry jam is sublime.

Da Giovanni ⑯

Pza Campo de' Fiori, 39

🚌 Bus to Corso Vittorio Emanuele II/tram to V. Arenula

Open: Mon–Sat 0800–2400

Giovanni's is probably the best takeaway pizzeria in the Campo de' Fiori area. Try the pizza *a taglio* with courgette flowers – it tastes as good as it looks!

Norcineria Viola (Antica Norcineria) ⑯

Pza Campo de' Fiori, 43C

🚌 Bus to Corso Vittorio Emanuele II/tram to V. Arenula

A century-old *salumeria* always crowded with shoppers stocking up on top-quality cold cuts. Delicacies include mountain salami, *guanciale*, *pancetta* (kinds of smoked bacon) and all kinds of goodies to take home as a souvenir or to use as fillings for the pizza *bianca* which you

▲ *Salumeria*

▲ Campo de' Fiori

can buy next door at the Forno.

Le Piramidi ㉓

Vicolo del Gallo

Ⓑ Bus to Corso Vittorio Emanuele II

Open: Tue–Sun 1030–0100

Specialises in Middle-Eastern snacks and sweets – and pizza too. Tasty and good value, just around the corner from Campo de' Fiori.

La Strega ㉔

V. dei Banchi Nuovi, 21B

Website: www.lastrega.com

Ⓑ Bus to Corso Vittorio Emanuele II

Open: Tue–Sat (Mon pm only) 0900–1300, 1530–1930

Macrobiotic foods, vitamins imported from the US and natural cosmetics are all attractively displayed here.

Zì Fenizia ⑬

V. Sta Maria del Pianto, 64

Ⓑ Bus to Corso Vittorio Emanuele II

Open: daily, closed on Jewish holidays

Better known as the kosher pizzeria in the ghetto, this very popular eatery does excellent pizza *a taglio* (by the slice): no cheese on the toppings but delicious all the same.

Markets

Campo de' Fiori ⑯

Pza Campo de' Fiori

Ⓑ Bus to Corso Vittorio Emanuele II

Open: Mon–Sat 0600–1330

This most central, picturesque and historical market is by no means just devoted to flowers. Legend has it that the name, translating as field of flowers, comes from *Campus Florae* (the square of Flora) who was the Roman general Pompey's lover. Not especially cheap, but a feast of freshest produce which is also extremely photogenic. As with all markets, do be wary of pickpockets at all times.

Picnic sites

The market and excellent selection of delicatessens on the piazza, together with the bakeries near by, are perfect for gathering picnic supplies to take perhaps to **Piazza Mattei** Ⓐ, site of the lovely Tortoise Fountain (*Fontana delle Tartarughe*). Alternatively, stroll down to the Tiber or on to the lovely boat-shaped **Isola Tiberin** Ⓐ itself. Here you will find yourself joined by the native Romans who come to sunbathe along the river's banks and escape the traffic and crowds of the city.

Fast food

A city on the move

In a city so devoted to the pleasures of the table, fast food does not enjoy the same popularity as in many other European capitals. However, lunch – traditionally the biggest meal of the day – is now more likely to be grabbed by Romans in a bar-café or *tavola calda* (serving hot and cold foods) rather than making the commute home.

Alimentari (grocery stores/takeaways) do a roaring trade from around noon to 1330, after which they close for their lunch. Here you can get *panini* (rolls), sandwiches or slices of pizza *bianca* (plain, salted, oiled pizza) with your choice of excellent fillings. Amongst the best are **Frontoni** in Trastevere (*see page 72*) and **Il Forno**, around Piazza Navona (*see page 19*). Outward appearances can be very deceptive in Rome: often the little hole in the wall can deliver the most gastronomic of delights and one such is **Fratelli Paladini** (*see page 25*) which, despite its rundown exterior, serves homemade pizza bianca by the slice (*a taglio*). In the ghetto, **Zì Fenizia** is Rome's only kosher pizzeria outlet (*see page 35*). Here Aunty Fenizia serves over 40 delicious flavours – without cheese – try her speciality *con alciotti e indivia* (anchovies and endive).

Tavole calde and *rosticcerie* (spit-roasts) are good value too, especially as you don't have to pay extra to sit down. In Testaccio, **Volpetti Più** (*see page 13*) is amongst the best, where you can get pasta, vegetable and meat dishes as well as pizza *a taglio*, washed down by good wine at *enoteca* prices. Near the opera, **Er Buchetto** (*V. del Viminale, 2F; ✆ 06 488 3031; open: 0900–2100, closed Sun and Sat pm*) specialises in roast baby piglet (*porchetta*) – deliciously aromatic meat with crackling sliced into thick country bread or rolls (*le rosette*).

Whilst most of the city's food is Roman and regional Italian, there is a better choice here than any other Italian city for

▲ Fast food bar

international and ethnic cuisine – although even then it is limited. The only Indian takeaway rejoices in its self-explanatory title: **Indian Fast Food** (*V. Mamainani, 11; ✆ 06 446 0792;* Ⓜ *metro to Vittorio; open: 0930–2200, closed Sun;* ❶). Located just off Piazza Vittorio, it's a great place for samosas and you can eat in too. If Egyptian food is more your style, **Shawerma Express** (*V. Calatafimi, 7; ✆ 06 481 8791;* Ⓜ *bus to Termini; open: daily 1100–2400;* ❶) serves tasty couscous and kebabs with pitta bread. Just around the corner from Campo de' Fiori, **Le Piramidi** (*see page 35*) has excellent Middle-Eastern light bites, pizzas and sweets.

There are over 100 Chinese restaurants in the city where service is usually speedy – but be wary of over-salted offerings. Amongst the best is **Golden Crown** (*V. in Arcione, 85; ✆ 06 678 6093;* ❶–❶❶), centrally located between the Palazzo del Quirinale and Via del Tritone. **Hasekura** (*V. dei Serpenti, 27;* Ⓜ *bus to V. Nazionale; open: lunch and dinner, closed Sun;* ❶–❶❶) is the best value of Rome's Japanese restaurants with good *tempura* or sushi: the set-price lunch menu is particularly good value. At Trastevere's **ATM** (*V. della Penitenzia, 7; ✆ 06 6830 7053;* Ⓜ *bus to Lungotevere Farnesina; open: evenings, closed Mon;* ❶–❶❶) you will find a very fashionable sushi bar, full of ambience, and the added attraction of it staying open late. Recalling Italy's past colonies, there is a range of Somali, Ethiopian and Eritrean eateries serving tasty, usually spicy, fare, mostly centred on the Termini area. Try **Africa** (*V. Gaeta, 26; ✆ 06 494 1077;* Ⓜ *bus to Termini; open: all day, closed Mon;* ❶–❶❶) for something refreshingly different. *Spriss* (spicy beef with onion and chilli) is a delicious speciality and vegetarians are catered too. It opens early for breakfast and closes at around midnight.

If you have a yearning for burgers then you will be pleased to discover that Rome is not a **McDonald's**-free zone! The best located of all is on the Piazza della Rotonda facing the Pantheon; others are on the piazzas della Repubblica and Spagna and in Viale di Trastevere, between piazzas Mastai and Sonnino. New York-style diner, **Jeff Flynn's** (*Vle dei Parioli, 103C*) does good burgers, steaks, French fries and real American apple pie. Should you need to be reminded of the taste of fish and chips and baked beans, seek out **Marconi** (*V. di Sta Prassede, 9, opposite Sta Maria Maggiore*). But for a true Roman experience go to **Filletti di Baccalà** (*see page 30*) Named after their speciality, fried fillets of cod, this delicious snack is one of the city's most traditional dishes … when in Rome!

> **Lunch is now more likely to be grabbed by Romans in a bar-café or tavola calda rather than making the commute home.**

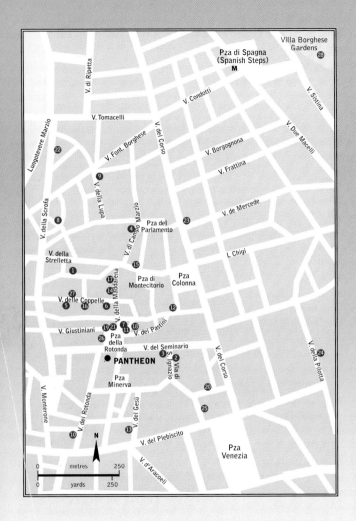

Piazza della Rotonda

Around the piazza and the Pantheon are some of Rome's most fêted restaurants – especially for seafood – which are both excellent and expensive. The area is also noteworthy for creative regional Italian cuisine and for the city's best ice cream.

PIAZZA DELLA ROTONDA
Restaurants

Il Bacaro ❶

V. degli Spagnoli, 27

✆ 06 686 4110

Ⓜ Metro A to Spagna

Open: Mon–Sat (also lunch May, June and Sept) 2000–2400

Reservations recommended

All credit cards accepted

Creative cuisine

€€

A stone's throw from the Pantheon, this tiny restaurant in an ivy-clad alleyway is a popular and romantic spot. The good wine list is complemented by imaginative, flavour-some cuisine including homemade pasta and a delicious combination of *radicchio* stuffed with gorgonzola. Main courses have an emphasis on meat – the warm *carpaccio* of beef is especially good. Reasonably priced.

Il Buco ❷

V. di Sant'Ignazio, 8

✆ 06 679 3298

Ⓜ Bus to Corso di Rinascimento

Open: Tue–Sun 1230–1600, 1900–2400

Reservations unnecessary

All credit cards accepted

No smoking area

Tuscan cuisine

€–€€

Established in 1891 as a tiny hole-in-the-wall (*buco*), this is now a big, bustling restaurant but remains faithful to its Tuscan origins and attentive service. Good for robust appetites and especially for the huge Florentine steaks and traditional *crostini* with liver pâté.

Le Due Colonne ❸

V. del Seminario, 122 (off Pza di San Ignazio)

✆ 06 678 1449

Ⓜ Bus to Corso di Rinascimento

Open: daily 1200–1500, 1900–2400

Reservations unnecessary

All credit cards accepted

Mediterranean cuisine

€–€€

On the street connecting the Pantheon and Sant'Ignazio, this well-placed restaurant is faithful to its name with two ancient Roman-style columns and a lovely old fountain. Spanish as well as Italian flavours feature, with an emphasis on

▲ Piazza della Rotonda

seafood: particularly good are the grilled squid and also the giant prawns with tomatoes.

Da Gino

Vicolo Rosini, 4 (Pza del Parlamento)

📞 06 687 3434

🚌 Bus to V. del Corso

Open: Mon–Sat 1245–1500, 2000–2230

Reservations recommended

No credit cards accepted

Cucina romana

€€

Old, atmospheric Roman trattoria which is extremely popular and conveniently placed (at Parliament Square) for politicians and journalists. Specials include homemade soups, *ossobuco*, *baccalà*, tripe and *gnocchi*, rotated on a daily basis. The wall frescos are perhaps a little kitsch and the lighting bright, but the regular clientele shows its enduring appeal.

Maccheroni ❺

Pza delle Coppelle, 44

📞 06 6830 7895

🚌 Bus to Corso del Rinascimento

Open: Mon–Sat 1300–1500, 2000–2400

Reservations unnecessary

All credit cards accepted

Italian home cooking

€–€€

See your food being prepared in the kitchens of this relatively new eatery, which proves very popular with young, local office workers. Set just off the

pretty square, inside the walls are smart and panelled and the counters long and marble. There are tables outdoors and the atmosphere is young and buzzy and the Italian home-style food mostly reliable.

Quinzi e Gabrieli ❻

V. delle Coppelle, 6

📞 06 687 9389

🚌 Bus to Corso del Rinascimento

Open: 1930–2330, closed Sun

Reservations essential

All credit cards accepted

Seafood

€€€

This Michelin-starred haven for fish lovers is probably Rome's top seafood restaurant and amongst the best in the whole of Italy. The house speciality of spaghetti with lobster is exquisite, as is the *carpaccio* (raw seafood) of sea bass, swordfish and shrimp. It all comes at a price, but the quality and service is faultless under the watchful eye of partners Alberto Quinzi and Enrico Gabrieli. Try to leave room for the superb puddings, especially the deliciously light mandarin sorbet (*sorbetto al mandarino*).

La Rosetta ❼

V. della Rosetta, 8/9

📞 06 6830 8841/06 686 1002

🚌 Bus to Corso del Rinascimento

Open: 1300–1500, 2000–2330, closed Sun and Sat lunch

Reservations essential

All credit cards accepted

Seafood

€€€

Many say that this is Rome's best fish restaurant. It has a coveted Michelin star and the members of the Riccioli family have run this elegant temple to seafood since the late 1960s. *Linguine con astice e gamberi* (homemade pasta with lobster and prawns) is superb, and the menu features just about every fish known to the Mediterranean – and more besides. Delicate improvisations of fruit and oils are used in marinades. Puddings include a chocoholic's delight – sublime *torta al cioccolato e cassatina*.

Sangallo ❽

Vicolo della Vaccarella, 11A

📞 06 686 5549

🚌 Bus to Corso del Rinascimento

Open: 1945–2230, closed Sun

Reservations essential

All credit cards accepted

Seafood

€€€

This is a small, elegant restaurant where olive oil and truffles feature alongside the fresh fish specialities. The salt-crusted sea bass (*spigola al sale*) is simplistically tasty and there are meat and vegetarian dishes on offer too. The whole emphasis is on simple preparation, complemented by an extensive wine list.

El Toulà ⑨

V. della Lupa, 29B

✆ 06 687 3498

Bus to V. della Scrofa

Open: Tue–Fri 1200–1500, 1930–2300, Mon–Sat 1930–2300

Reservations essential

All credit cards accepted

Sophisticated Venetian and international

€€€

Elegance, beautiful décor and haute cuisine make this one of Rome's top restaurants. Befitting its origins, there is one section of the menu devoted to Venetian specialities such as calf's liver (*fegato alla veneziana*). Other delicacies include *risotto al prosecco* – deliciously light in sparkling white wine – and many excellent fish dishes. An extensive and expensive wine list ensures a well-heeled clientele, but the beautiful ambience and excellent food make dining here an unforgettable experience.

Vecchia Locanda ⑩

Vicolo Sinibaldi, 2

✆ 06 6880 2831

Bus to Corso Vittorio Emanuele II

Open: Mon–Sat 1230–1500, 1900–2400

Reservations recommended

All credit cards accepted

Creative Italian

€–€€

Excellent pasta dishes, as well as fresh fish, are served at this small, family-run Ligurian restaurant near to the Pantheon. Try the delicious *stringozzi con gorgonzola e radicchio* (pasta with the king of blue cheeses and *radicchio*) or *porcini* mushroom crêpes.

PIAZZA DELLA ROTONDA
Bars, cafés and pubs

Caffè di Rienzo ⑪

Pza della Rotonda, 8/9

🚌 Bus to Corso del Rinascimento

Open: daily 0700–0100

Opposite the Pantheon, this is the best café on the piazza where you can sit at a pavement table with a cooling *granità* or enjoy a pizza or pasta – or something more substantial. Inside, the walls are inlaid with the same kind of marble found on the floor of the Pantheon.

La Caffetiera ⑫

Pza di Pietra, 65

🚌 Bus to Corso di Rinascimento

Open: Mon–Sat 0700–2100

All kinds of light snacks including sandwiches, slices of quiche and savoury tarts, Neapolitan-style ice cream delights, even afternoon tea, are happily consumed in this bustling, carefully restored café. Prices are reasonable too, given its location near the Pantheon.

Enoteca Corsi ⑬

V. del Gesù, 88

🚌 Bus to V. del Plebiscito

Open: lunch only, closed Sun

▲ Gelateria della Palma

Between Corso Vittorio Emanuele II and Piazza della Pigna, this wine bar-trattoria is more like a working man's café where you can eat well and cheaply. Especially recommended is the *tonno e fagioli* (tuna and beans). Try to get there early, around noon, as by 1230 it tends to fill up very quickly.

Gelateria della Palma 14

V. della Maddalena 20/23

🚌 Bus to Pza della Rotonda

Open: daily 0800–0200

Just behind the Pantheon, this buzzing ice cream parlour, designer café and cocktail bar has a huge selection of over 100 flavours of the freshest (unsweetened) *gelati*, including fig, pomegranate, and even avocado. Many say this is the city's best ice cream parlour and it also features frozen yoghurts, mousses and delicious cakes, chocolate and technicoloured serve-yourself confectionery.

Giolitti 15

V. Uffici del Vicario, 40

Website: *www.giolitti.it*

🚌 Bus to V. del Corso,

Open: Tue–Sat 0900–1300

Opened in 1900, this legendary teashop-*gelateria* is famous for its wonderful ice creams, boasting 70 flavours; try the *marron glacé* and *frutti di bosci*. It also

serves good pastries and cakes and the main bar has long been a port of call on the evening *passeggiata* – the time to stroll, see and be seen. Popular with everyone from Roman locals, families and tourists to construction workers and parliamentary officials.

Ned Kelly 16

V. delle Coppelle,13

🚌 Bus to Corso di Rinascimento

Open: daily until late

Buzzing Australian style pub-bar serving plenty of long, cool lager and other beers on tap. Beer drinking is getting more popular with the young Romans and this is amongst the favourite haunts.

La Scaletta 17

V. della Maddalena, 46/49

🚌 Bus to Pza della Rotonda

Open: daily 1000–0030

Wine bar and *birreria*, owned by **Myosotis** (*see page 20*). As you would expect from its parent restaurant, it is excellent value with a wide selection, plus being well located near the Pantheon.

La Tazza d'Oro 18

V. degli Orfani, 82/84

🚌 Bus to V. del Corso

Open: Mon–Sat 0700–2030

'The Golden Cup' is superbly located overlooking the Pantheon; some say this is the best coffee in Rome, and the rich aroma draws in

many regulars and tourists for their caffeine fix. Try the excellent *granità di caffè* (iced coffee) with *panna* – lashings of whipped cream. Perhaps buy some of the house coffee which is sold in hessian bags as a souvenir.

Tempio Bar 19

Pza della Rotonda, 16

🚌 Bus to Pza della Rotonda

Open: Thu–Tue 0700–0100

This bar, *gelateria* and *birreria* enjoys an excellent location with great views of the Pantheon, where good sandwiches, pizzas and snacks are reasonably priced. But remember that prices are roughly doubled if you elect to sit at a table rather than stand.

Trinity College 20

V. del Collegio Romano, 6

🚌 Bus to V. del Corso

Open: daily 1130–0300

This central pub is opposite the Ministry for Cultural Heritage, so, as you'd expect, a lot of the employees use it as their local. Other patrons include the students of the Visconti high school and a lot of curious tourists.

PIAZZA DELLA ROTONDA
Shops, markets and picnic sites

Shops

L'Antica Salumeria ㉑

Pza della Rotonda, 4

🚌 Bus to Pza della Rotonda

Open: every day

This up-market deli which specialises in home deliveries is opposite the Pantheon Bar. You'll find everything here for the most sumptuous picnic, from salamis and hams to slices of pizza *romana* stuffed perhaps with tuna and tomato or *prosciutto crudo e fichi* (raw ham and figs).

Buccone ㉒

V. di Ripetta, 19/20

🚌 Bus to Pza Augusto Imperatore

Open: daily 0900–2030 (to 2400 Wed–Sat)

Very select wine and spirit shop housed in a 17th-century palazzo, all divided up into regions, from the very cheap to a million lire's worth. There is also an *enoteca* which serves good and not overly expensive snacks.

Cíao ㉓

V. del Corso/V. Convertite

🚌 Bus to V. del Corso

Open: closed Mon

Good-value self-service restaurant and a great selection of takeaway pizza *a taglio* served in gargantuan slices. This is one of the cheapest and most cheerful establishments in the area and is extremely popular.

Confetteria Moriondo e Garigli ㉔

V. della Pilotta, 2

🚌 Bus to V. del Corso

Open: Mon–Sat 0930–1300, 1530–1930

No credit cards accepted

All the delicious chocolates are made on the premises in this family-run, beautifully presented chocolate confectionery. For the ultimate romantic gesture, do as the Romans do and have

▲ L'Antica Salumeria

your special gift enrobed in handmade chocolate hearts or eggs for Valentine's day, Easter or whenever – you almost certainly will not be disappointed. In the weeks before Christmas and Easter the shop stays open at lunchtime.

La Corte 25

V. della Gatta, 1 (off Pza del Collegio Romano)

🚍 Bus to Pza Venezia or V. del Corso

Open: 0930–1300, 1700–1930, closed Sat pm and Sun

A tiny shop specialising in smoked fish owned by Englishman John Fort. Especially good are the salmon and swordfish (*spada*). Extremely popular with the Romans.

Cremeria Monteforte 26

V. della Rotonda, 22

🚍 Bus to Pza della Rotonda

Open: 0930–2400, closed Mon

Tiny ice cream shop opposite the Pantheon offers 30 different flavours all made on the premises. The stracciatella and *cassata siciliana* are deserving of the parlour's advertising slogan, 'the best'.

Fiocco di Neve 11

V. del Pantheon, 51

🚍 Bus to Pza della Rotonda

Open: daily

Specialises in ice cream where crunchy rice is a

delicious addition to the many traditional flavours. The small cones really are small and not over-generous with the delicious contents. It also serves good cakes and pastries.

Markets

Piazza delle Coppelle 27

🚍 Bus to Pza della Rotonda

Open: Mon–Sat 0600–1400

Some say this little market is the most picturesque of all, nestling right in the heart of the city, near the Pantheon. Flowers, fruit and all kinds of comestibles are on offer, beautifully displayed, adding a lovely splash of colour to the heart of the city. Small is certainly beautiful here.

Picnic sites

As this is the main financial district of Rome with the Stock Exchange and banking headquarters, the number of open spaces for a picnic are limited. However, you will always find the area around the Pantheon an exciting hub of activity, a good place to buy an ice cream from **Giolitti** or its rival the **Gelateria della Palma** (*see page 43*). It's for you to decide which is the best!

Villa Borghese Gardens 28

🚍 Bus to Corso d'Italia

Open: dawn to dusk daily

Rome's largest public park is a gorgeous pleasure garden with statues, pavilions and fountains, originally laid out in the 17th century by Cardinal Scipione Borghese. Today it provides a cool retreat from the city, perfect for a relaxing picnic.

Business dining

Attentive not servile

Although Milan is Italy's main business centre, Rome's business population is a thriving one with a wonderful range of restaurants from which to choose. It is always a good idea to reconfirm any appointments that you make, as Italians can be notorious for not turning up and tend to be rather relaxed about time-keeping. However, polite formality in addressing a business associate is very important and Italians tend to use correct titles all the time. It is not considered to be good etiquette to mix business talk with your meal – food is of paramount importance in Italy!

One of the best areas for business dining is north of Villa Borghese in the exclusive area of Parioli with its embassies and opulent town houses. It also has a big concentration of smart restaurants which are very popular with a business clientele.

The justly fêted **Relais Le Jardin at the Hotel Byron** (*V. G de Notaris, 5; ✆ 06 322 0404; reservations essential; all credit cards accepted;* ❶❷❸) has delicious Italian nouvelle cuisine in very elegant, romantic décor with faultless service.

Al Ceppo (*V. Panama, 2; ✆ 06 841 9696; open: lunch and dinner, closed Mon; reservations essential; all credit cards accepted;* ❶❷–❶❷❸) offers creative cooking from the Marche region. Excellent meat is sourced from the pastureland of the Marche and cooked on the wood fire (after the restaurant's log symbol).

Meeting (*Vle Rossini, 44; ✆ 06 855 1048; open: lunch and dinner, closed Sun; reservations recommended; all credit cards accepted;* ❶❷) is a very smart restaurant perfect for a quick business lunch, but many people find themselves lingering longer.

Caminetto (*Vle dei Parioli, 89; ✆ 06 808 3946; open: lunch and dinner daily; reservations recommended; all credit cards accepted;* ❶❷) specialises in creative cooking with the emphasis on fish.

In Trastevere **Il Ciak** (*Vicolo del Cinque, 21; ✆ 06 589 4774; open: evenings, closed Mon; reservations recommended; all credit cards accepted;* ❶❷) is very popular with the media, where Tuscan specialities include *tagliata* (sliced fillet steak) and

▲ St Regis Grand

good sautéed seafood and ravioli, with efficient and friendly service overseen by the chef/patron.

In the centre of Rome, near the **Antico Caffè Greco** (*see page 62*), **El Toulà** (*see page 41*) is outstanding for its haute cuisine and tasteful atmosphere. Near Piazza Navona **Osteria dell'Ingegno** (*Pza della Pietra, 45; ℘ 06 678 0662; closed Sun; reservations essential; all credit cards accepted*) is a designer restaurant, relatively new on the scene.

Pierluigi (*Pza de'Ricci, 144; ℘ 06 686 1302; website: www.ristorante-pierluigi.com; ⊛ bus to Pza Farnese/V. Giulia; reservations recommended; all credit cards accepted;* ❶❶) is a solid, well-established Roman restaurant with excellent food, especially fish.

Around Campo de' Fiori **Camponeschi** (*see page 28*) is beautifully situated in the car-free Piazza Farnese and is especially favoured by diplomats, politicians and the glitterati.

The newly-opened **Rocco Forte Hotel de Russie** (*V. del Babuino, 9; ℘ 06 32 8881*) promises to be the ultimate in elegance and luxury with its bar and restaurant opening on to fabulous gardens. Just off the Via Veneto, **George's** (*see page 49*) offers a clubby atmosphere and discreet service from some of the most professional staff in Rome. The international cuisine is excellent: it boasts one of the city's finest wine cellars and has tables in the lovely garden.

▲ St Regis Grand

L'Ortica (*V. Flaminia Vecchia, 573, nr Villa Giulia; ℘ 06 333 8709; open: evenings, closed Sun; reservations recommended; all credit cards accepted;* ❶❶– ❶❶❶) focuses on excellent regional Italian cuisine, including Neapolitan and Genoese specialities that make this one of Rome's top restaurants and which is not exorbitantly priced. **La Terrazza dell'Hotel Eden** (*see page 51*) prefers modern Mediterranean cuisine, Roman specialities and a macrobiotic menu presided over by chef Enrico Derflingher, formerly of Kensington Palace.

The fabulous, newly restored **St Regis Grand** (*V. Vittorio Emanuele Orlando, 3; ℘ 06 47 091; website: www.luxurycollection.com/Grand Rome; open: daily; reservations essential; all credit cards accepted;* ❶❶❶) is legendary in elegance, hospitality and haute cuisine. The ancient rule imposed over a century ago by César Ritz still holds today: 'see without looking, hear without listening, be attentive but not servile'. Perfection indeed!

> **It is not considered to be good etiquette to mix business talk with your meal – food is of paramount importance in Italy!**

Via Veneto and Quirinale

The Via Veneto of the high society era may have lost its glamour, but there is still some very sophisticated dining around here. The Via Nazionale and Termini have a good sprinkling of ethnic restaurants and a wide range of different gourmet experiences.

VIA VENETO AND QUIRINALE
Restaurants

Cantina Cantarini ❶

Pza Sallustio, 12

Ø 06 485 528

🚍 Bus to V. XX Settembre

Open: Mon–Sat 1230–1530, 1930–2330

Reservations recommended

All credit cards accepted

Roman/Marche region

€–€€

Authentic taverna serving good simple dishes, where the menu changes from meat-based Roman and *marchigiana* (from the Marche region) speciali-ties to fish from Thursday to Saturday. Bustling atmosphere and slightly cramped seating but the food is palatable and the prices exceptionally reasonable.

Est!Est!Est! (Antica Pizzeria Fratelli Ricci) ❷

V. Genova, 32

Ø 06 488 1107

🚍 Bus to V. Nazionale

Open: Tue–Sun 1900–2400

Reservations recommended

💳 Eurocard

Pizzeria

€

Formica-topped tables, brisk, friendly service by waiters past the first flush of youth and queues of hungry locals testify to the popularity of one of Rome's oldest pizzerias. They also serve *filletti di baccalà* and various *fritti* in addition to good pasta and excellent *calzoni ripieni al forno* (folded-over pizzas). Named after the white wine,

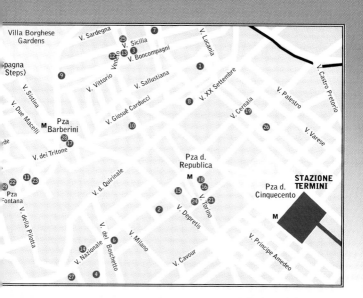

Est!Est!Est!, the house variety is served on draught from a former ice machine in what looks like an old wooden oven. Excellent value.

George's ❸

V. Marche, 7

✆ 06 4208 4575

🚌 Bus to V. Vittorio Veneto or Metro A to Barberini

Open: Mon–Sat 1230–1500, 1930–2400

Reservations essential

All credit cards accepted

International cuisine

❸❸❸

Just off the Via Veneto, this elegant restaurant in an 18th-century building has a faithful following, some of

▲ Est!Est!Est!

whom use it like a club, dropping in for a pre-dinner drink in the piano bar. But it would be a shame not to enjoy the excellent dishes served in the dining room amidst the crisp white linen and sparkling glassware. Dishes vary from smoked trout served with horseradish sauce to all kinds of meat and fish dishes. An added bonus is al fresco dining in the garden of a papal villa during the summer months.

Maharajah ④

V. dei Serpenti, 124
✆ 06 4747 144
🚍 Bus to V. Nazionale

Open: Mon–Sat and Sun evening 1230–1430, 1900–2330

Reservations unnecessary
All credit cards accepted
Indian-Punjabi

€€

In a city not noted for its wide choice of Indian restaurants, this is Rome's best. The tandoori oven serves excellent chicken tikka massala amongst many other spicier delights. There are also good value vegetarian and non-vegetarian fixed-price menus and delicious puddings.

Al Moro ⑤

Vicolo delle Bollette, 13

✆ 06 678 3495

🚍 Bus to V. del Corso

Open: Mon–Sat 1300–1530, 2000–2330

Reservations essential
No credit cards accepted
Cucina romana

€€

This bustling, always crowded trattoria near to the Trevi Fountain was Fellini's favourite restaurant in the 1960s. Owner Franco Romagnoli (il Moro) offers good traditional Roman cooking where specials include spaghetti *alla Moro* (a particularly tasty version of spaghetti *alla carbonara*) and delicious *baccalà*. There's excellent homemade bread and a very extensive wine list.

Il Quadrifoglio ⑥

V. del Boschetto, 19
✆ 06 482 6096
🚇 Metro B to Cavour
Open: Mon–Sat 1900–2400
Reservations recommended
All credit cards accepted
Southern Italian

€€

Warm southern hospitality featuring the cuisine of Campania, Naples and North Africa in this popular restaurant. Good selection of *antipasti* and excellent homemade pasta as well as meatballs and delicious grilled octopus. The puddings are amongst the best in Rome. A good wine list features wines mostly from Campania.

▲ Monte Quirinale

Le Sans Souci 7

V. Sicilia, 20

✆ 06 482 1814

🚇 Metro A to Barberini

Open: Tue–Sun 2000–0100

Reservations essential

All credit cards accepted

French-Italian

€€€

Very stylish restaurant, now Michelin-starred once again. Lavish ingredients, impeccably served, include home-made *foie gras* (*scallopa di foie gras fresco delle Landes*) and ravioli with Umbrian truffles (*tortelli ripieni ai due tartufi*). The lightest of soufflés come in vegetable or sweet variety and the wine list is excellent. Glamorous in every way, with prices to reflect a special evening out.

Taverna Flavia 8

V. Flavia, 9

✆ 06 4745 214/06 481 7787

🚇 Bus to V. XX Settembre

Open: Mon–Sat 1230–1500, 1930–2330, closed Sun

Reservations recommended

All credit cards accepted

Roman-Italian

€€

Once the centre of high society and famous for its patronage by the 1950s *Hollywood on the Tiber* crowd, the food remains as good as ever. Hearty dishes include *trippa alla romana* (tripe), but lighter alternatives include risotto with

scampi, savoury seafood salads or the inappropriately-named chicken breast 'Hitchcock style' – just the way he liked it! Always busy and, even if the glitterati are no longer in evidence, the signed celebrity photos on the walls certainly are.

La Terrazza dell'Hotel Eden 9

V. Ludovisi, 49

✆ 06 478 121

🚇 Metro A to Barberini

Open: daily 1230–1430, 1930–2230

Reservations recommended

All credit cards accepted

Italian–International

€€€

Faultless cuisine and service in one of Rome's top restaurants. The view from the fifth floor is pretty stunning too, with marvellous vistas over St Peter's. In addition to the à la carte menu there are two fixed-price menus featuring either Roman specialities or macrobiotic dishes. *Branzino al sale, olive nere, origano e patate* (sea bass baked

in a black olive sea crust) is one of Chef Enrico Derfligher's delicious signature dishes. A truly gourmet experience at haute cuisine prices.

Tullio 10

V. San Nicola de Tolentino, 26

✆ 06 474 55 60

🚇 Metro A to Barberini

Open: 1230–1500, 1930–2300, closed Sun

Reservations recommended

All credit cards accepted

Tuscan cuisine

€€

Fresh fish, the best mozzarella cheese, *porcini* mushrooms and Florentine steaks are some of the specialities here at one of Rome's very best restaurants for Tuscan cuisine. The rustic atmosphere, courteous and speedy service make this a very popular spot, especially at lunchtime, with journalists and politicians. The excellent food, which also includes Roman specialities, is reasonably priced and served in extremely generous portions.

VIA VENETO AND QUIRINALE
Bars, cafés and pubs

Bar Gelateria Fontana di Trevi ⓫

Pza di Trevi, 90

Ⓜ Metro A to Barberini

Open: all day

Perfectly located for the city's largest and most spectacular fountain, the glorious Trevi. Enjoy a milkshake or espresso, a delicious zabaglione ice cream or spoil yourself with a huge banana split (whipped cream optional).

Café de Paris ⓬

V. Vittorio Veneto, 90

Ⓜ Bus to V. Vittorio Veneto

Open: 0800–2000, closed Wed

Located across the street from **Café Doney** (see below), both these cafés had their heyday in the 1950s in the high society era. This café was more for the streetwise, whilst Doney was more up-market. Still hugely popular, especially in the summer: if you can, find a table outside, as the inside is past its prime.

Café Doney ⓭

V. Vittorio Veneto, 145

Ⓜ Bus to V. Vittorio Veneto

Open: 0800–0100, closed Wed

This famous café was started by a family of English pastry cooks in the 1940s and, a decade later, was the haunt of the Cinecittà set, including Marcello Mastroianni, Anita Ekberg and Ava Gardner, as well as the elite of Roman cultural society. Nowadays you're more likely to rub shoulders with Japanese camera-toting tourists, but it is still a good venue for a coffee 'on the hoof' or a leisurely drink on the eternally popular Via Veneto.

Café Renault ⓮

V. Nazionale, 183B

Ⓜ Bus to V. Nazionale

Open: daily until late

With its own radio station, ultra trendy chrome interior and video screens, this huge

café is the place to see and be seen. The pace quickens late at night to the thump of loud music. The café also has its own car to ferry customers to and from the piazzas della Repubblica and Venezia – a Renault Espace, of course.

Flann O'Brien Pub  15

V. Napoli, 29

🚌 Bus to V. Nazionale

Open: daily 0700–0130

Authentic Dublin décor in this very busy, friendly hostelry which is more than just a pub. Breakfast on a cappuccino and *cornetto*, lunch on traditional Italian specialities and in the afternoon take tea with sticky homemade pastries in the tearoom. The tempo goes up a notch with Irish coffee later in the afternoon and Guinness goes down well at any time!

Goffredo Chirra Enoteca 16

V. Torino, 133

🚌 Bus to V. Nazionale

Open: All day until late

Good late-night spot for snacks and a glass of wine. Also a grocery shop with its shelves piled high with wine bottles and delicious edibles.

Harry's Bar 13

V. Vittorio Veneto, 150

🚌 Bus to V. Vittorio Veneto

Open: 1100–0200, closed Sun

Harry's bars are a permanent fixture for most Italian cities and this Roman version is chic and sophisticated. A new, air-conditioned café is open from May to November dishing up pleasant food, or you can linger outside over a long cool drink. The piano bar opens every night with live music starting at 2300.

Planet Hollywood 17

V. del Tritone, 118

🚇 Metro A to Barberini

Open: daily until late

Very popular with the young set so if you need a shot of American razzmatazz, this is the place to come. Especially well patronised are the happy hours from 1600 to 2000 every weekday!

Target Grill & Pizza 18

V. Torino, 33

🚌 Bus to V. XX Settembre

Open: Mon–Sat and Sun evening 1200–1500, 1900–0030

You can't miss the clever designer lighting in this busy cocktail bar which also has two dining rooms. An open large grill offers a big selection of fresh meat, especially steaks, and fish, as well as good pizzas and a buffet.

Trimani Wine Bar 19

V. Cernaia, 37B

🚌 Bus to V. XX Settembre

Open: daily 1130–1500, 1730–0030

Enjoy a glass or two of wine chosen from an excellent choice of Italian regional wines, accompanied by tasty snacks – pasta, cold cuts, *torte salate* (savoury tarts) and soups. Extremely popular, as you would expect from its status as the offshoot of the **Trimani Enoteca**, Rome's oldest and perhaps best wine shop (*see page 55*).

VIA VENETO AND QUIRINALE
Shops, markets and picnic sites

Shops

L'Antico Forno ⑳
V. delle Muratte, 8/Pza Trevi

🚇 Metro A to Barberini

Open: 0700–2100, closed Thu pm (opening times change in winter)

Old style bakery-delicatessen just a coin's throw from the Trevi Fountain. Here you can buy seafood salad, rice and fresh rolls with or without fillings. In view of its location, you'll be pleasantly surprised by efficient service and reasonable prices.

Enoteca Vinicolo Angelini ㉑
V. Viminale, 62

🚌 Bus to Termini

Open: daily 0900–1400, 1600–2100

This well-stocked wine merchant sells spirits and wine from all over the world, as well as Italy. Good Frascati can be bought from the barrel.

Farmacia Pesci ㉒
Pza Fontana di Trevi, 89

🚇 Metro A to Barberini

Open: Mon–Sat 0830–1930, closed Sat pm and Sun

More of an apothecary than a run-of-the-mill chemist, with porphyry vases, ceramic urns of herbs, medicines and wooden furnishings dating back over 300 years. However, should you have overindulged on gourmet or liquid delights, their remedies are effective and up to date.

Gelateria San Crispino ㉓
Corner of Pza Fontana di Trevi/V. della Panetteria, 54

🚇 Metro A to Barberini

Open: all day, closed Tue

Just around the corner from the Trevi fountain, the natural ingredients of what some say is the best ice cream in Italy, come in a variety of delicious, natural flavours at this sparkling *gelateria*. The aged armagnac and Sicilian orange sorbets are especially good.

Gran Caffè Strega ㉔
Pza Viminale, 27–31

🚌 Bus to V. Nazionale

Open: daily 0600–2400

Delicious cakes and ice cream are on sale here. It is also good for an eat-in good-value snack or lunch, with a *forno a legna* (wood oven) churning out the delicious pizzas.

Hard Rock Café ⑬
V. Vittorio Veneto, 62A

🚌 Bus to V. Vittorio Veneto

Open: daily until late

An institution for the last 25 years, this fast diner has a restaurant, bar and a boutique with

▲ *Enoteca*

ideas for stocking up on souvenirs.

Museum Shop 14

V. Nazionale, 185

🚌 Bus to V. Nazionale

Open: daily

You'll discover all kinds of original souvenirs here, including brightly painted espresso cups – good value and they really do make your coffee back home taste more authentic!

Palombi 25

V. Veneto, 114

🚌 Bus to V. Vittorio Veneto

Open: daily except Thu pm

Discover a paradise for pasta, with a huge selection of recipes, including fennel, avocado and even radish variations, all sold in a plethora of shapes, sizes and colours; the fresh pasta is especially good. (It is worth noting that fresh pasta will keep for up to two weeks if it is not encased in plastic and is left in the open, unwrapped).

Trimani Enoteca 26

V. Goito, 20

🚌 Bus to V. XX Settembre

Open: Mon–Sat 0830–1330, 1530–2000, Sun 1000–1300, 1600–1930

Founded in 1821, many would claim that this is not only the oldest, but also the best wine shop in Rome. Should you be tempted to buy in bulk, they will deliver anywhere in the world.

Picnic sites

Piazza Barberini 28 (by the two baroque fountains)

🚇 Metro to Barberini

The Triton Fountain and Bee Fountain are two beautiful, baroque Bernini creations – an inspirational setting.

Trevi Fountain 29

🚇 Metro A to Barberini

One of the great pleasures of Rome is to find your way through the twisting little streets to emerge at this glorious fountain which seems to take up the whole piazza. If you can, find a seat or return after dark with your picnic for a moonlit feast, when the sight is even more entrancing.

Villa Aldobrandini Gardens 27

V. Panisperna (entrance at V. Mazzarino, 1)

Open: dawn to dusk daily

🚇 Metro to Cavour

Hidden behind a high wall running along the V. Nazionale, these gardens are a haven of peace and calm in the city centre. Shady specimen trees fringe formal lawns, terraces and gravel paths. The villa itself belongs to the government and houses a law library, which is not open to the public. Seek out a bench and admire the wonderful vistas from your viewpoint of ten metres above street level.

La dolce vita

Calling all those with a sweet tooth

Rome's legendary street, the Via Veneto, shot to fame in the 1960s when it featured in *La Dolce Vita*, the best known film of Franco Fellini, the satirical film director and observer of Roman life. The glitzy street and the Trevi Fountain were the setting for Anita Ekberg's and Marcello Mastroianni's famous moonlit frolic. Even the name '*paparazzo*' originated here; it was the surname of the photojournalist in the film, modelled on Italian photographer Tazio Secchiaroli.

Whilst you are unlikely to spot any of the glitterati or paparazzi here today, the Via's oldest hotel, the **Excelsior**, continues to reinvent itself and has recently been lavishly refurbished (*Hotel Westin*

▲ Hotel Excelsior

Excelsior, V. Vittorio Veneto, 125; ✆ 06 470 82688). When it first opened in 1906, the Via Veneto was just a suburban street, a connecting road for carriages through the Roman countryside. By the 1920s the Excelsior had become one of Rome's leading hotels and has hosted everyone from Prince Ranier and Princess Grace of Monaco to the Rolling Stones. Amidst the opulent marble and chandeliers, it is still a wonderful place to take tea and *dolci* (pastries).

Just along from the Excelsior is **Café Doney** (*see page 52*), a great place at any time of the day to relax on the Via Veneto, people-watch and enjoy the legacy passed down by the family of English pastry cooks who founded it in the 1940s. The **Café de Paris** (*see page 52*) is another former bastion of Roman high society.

Nowadays, the glitterati are more likely to be found in the **Bar della Pace** (*see page 22*), around the Campo de' Fiori, in Trastevere, Testaccio or in the San Lorenzo area. Near the very smart Via Margutta, **La Caffettiera**'s (*see page 42*) delicious confections, including rum baba and *sfogliatella*, are mouth-wateringly sublime. These paper-thin layers of pastry are the ancestors of millefeuilles, each laden with butter, sugar, orange peel, cinnamon and ricotta.

Yet pastry shops did not appear on the Roman scene until well into the 18th century: pastries and cakes (*dolci*) were made at home or ordered from convents. However, it was not long before almond cake spread from the Jewish ghetto to all the tables of Rome. The speciality today of **Il Forno del Ghetto** (*see page 34*) is the unforgettable ricotta and damson tart.

There has always been a rivalry between Neapolitan and Sicilian pastry cooks for you to choose between them, if you can! **Pasticceria Bella Napoli** (*Corso Vittorio Emanuele II, 246*) has glorious *sfogliatelle* and excellent traditional Christmas, carnival and Easter cakes (*pastiera*), all very rich with orange-flower water, ricotta, citrus peel and whole grains of wheat. Near Piazza della Repubblica, Sicilian **Dagnino** (*Galleria Esedra, V. E Orlando, 75; open: daily*) is always popular for its crisp *cannoli siciliani* filled with ricotta and that Sicilian speciality *cassata*.

The traditional Roman breakfast of cappuccino and a good *cornetto* is not easy to find nowadays. An authentic *cornetto* (the Italian version of a croissant) should be low in fat and sugar, light and yeasty and made even more delicious when filled with whipped cream (*panna*). For the best go to **Bernasconi** (*see page 32*).

The Roman pastry business has never known the meaning of

▲ Caffè Dolce Vita

the word 'recession'. Generations of Romans have stopped off at the best pastry shop in the neighbourhood on their way home from Sunday Mass for a tray of *pastarelle*. Some of the best *pasticcerie* are still in the residential areas of Rome where the elegantly coiffed come to buy their cakes for that important dinner party or celebration – an important part of the *bella figura* style! **Antonini** (*see page 83*) in Prati is one of Rome's best, together with **Ruschena** (*see page 83*), also in the Prati district near Piazza Cavour.

... each laden with butter, sugar, orange peel, cinnamon and ricotta ...

The characteristic area of Trastevere is one of the hotspots for the new era of the glitterati and bohemian-style setters and is rich in its *dolci*, too. **Valzani** (*V. del Moro, 37*) specialises in mouth-watering chocolate cakes, whilst **Pasticceria Trastevere** (*V. Natale del Grande, 49/50*) has a great range of all kinds of cakes and biscuits. Right on the market square, **Sacchetti** (*Pza San Cosimato, 61/2*) has homemade *cornetti* and *sfogliatelle romane*, oozing with delicious ricotta cheese.

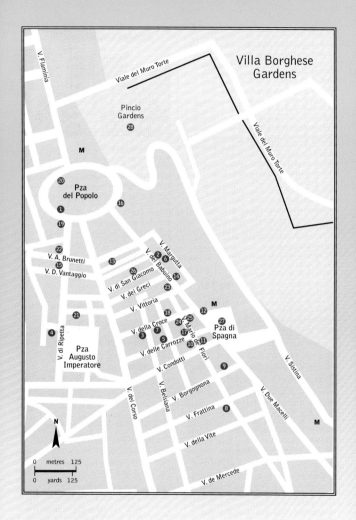

Il Tridente

The area from the Piazza del Popolo running down the three streets of 'the trident' is a tourist mecca, yet the local restaurant owners have not, in general, increased their prices accordingly. Even around the corner from the Spanish Steps you can eat extremely well at moderate prices.

IL TRIDENTE
Restaurants

Dal Bolognese ❶

Pza del Popolo, 1/2

✆ 06 361 1426

🚇 Metro A to Flaminio

Open: Tue–Sun 1245–1500, 2015–2330

Reservations essential

All credit cards accepted

Regional Italian

💰💰💰

This famous, designer restaurant proves very popular with media types, artists and politicians. The cuisine is from the northern Emilia-Romagana region which is based on the solid Bolognese tradition, yet it is not too heavy. The selection of four pastas, *misto de pasta*, is skilfully prepared and beautifully presented, as are the veal cutlets *bolognese*.

Edy ❷

Vicolo del Babuino, 4

✆ 06 3600 1738

🚇 Bus to V. del Babuino

Open: Mon–Sat 1200–1530, 1900–0200

Reservations recommended

All credit cards accepted

Cucina romana

💰💰

Authentic Roman cooking where the menu changes with the seasons. Excellent, delicate tagliatelle, light ravioli and the house

speciality, spaghetti *al cartoccio con frutti di mare* – a delicious seafood and spaghetti dish baked and served in a foil packet. Reasonable prices too in this pleasant, atmospheric trattoria.

Fiaschetteria Beltramme da Cesaretto ❸

V. della Croce, 39

No telephone

🚇 Metro A to Spagna

Open: Mon–Sat 1215–1500, 1930–2300

Reservations not allowed

No credit cards accepted

Roman cooking

💰–💰💰

Generations of artists have eaten here in this lovely old historical monument with an outside courtyard, just around the corner from the Spanish Steps. The walls are adorned with their works from the last century. Rub shoulders with fellow diners from every walk of life as you tuck into traditional Roman family cooking.

Gusto ❹

Pza Augusto Imperatore, 9

✆ 06 322 6273

🚇 Metro to Flaminio

Open: Tue–Sun 1230–1500, 2000–0200

Reservations recommended

💳 💳 American Express

Italian-Oriental fusion

💰–💰💰

On the ground floor a pizzeria offers a good selection of homemade pasta, salads, grilled dishes and, of course, pizza. Upstairs, minimalist décor complements the modern fusion cuisine which delivers such interesting marriages as stir-fried spaghetti in a wok with *al dente* vegetables or prawns *tempura* style. Not for the purist, but the innovative dishes and ambience have made this a popular, reasonably priced 'concept' restaurant.

Hostaria al 31 ❺

V. delle Carrozze, 31

✆ 06 678 6127

🚇 Metro A to Spagna

Open: 1215–1500, 1915–2230, closed Sun

Reservations recommended

All credit cards accepted

Roman cuisine

💰–💰💰

Very popular with tourists and locals, this pine-panelled modest restaurant specialises in traditional Roman food. The staples include carciofi alla romana (whole artichokes cooked with herbs) and

▲ The Spanish Steps

good lamb variations. Prices are very reasonable, especially given the location in an exclusive area.

Margutta Vegetariano ⑥

V. Margutta, 118	
⊘ 06 3265 9577	
🚍 Bus to Pza del Popolo	
Open: daily 1100–2400	
Reservations unnecessary	
🔲 💳 ⓓ Eurocard	
Mediterranean-Vegetarian	
€€	

This arty, airy, plant-filled restaurant is more than Rome's original temple to vegetarianism. Located on the exclusive Via Margutta, it is an open house for everyone wanting to relax over a book or a cup of tea in the piano bar. The food is both excellent and imaginative, ranging from pasta and salads to

soufflés. All wines, ciders and beers are organically produced. Taking brunch here from 1100 to 1500 is very popular and is a recent addition to the Roman dining scene.

Otello alla Concordia ⑦

V. della Croce, 81	
⊘ 06 679 1178	
🚇 Metro A to Spagna	
Open: Mon–Sat 1230–1500, 1930–2300	
Reservations recommended	
All credit cards accepted	
Roman food	
€–€€	

In one of Rome's most popular restaurants just off the Spanish Steps, robust traditional dishes such as spaghetti *alle vongole* and *abbacchio arrosto* (baby roast lamb) appear on the menu alongside grilled

and sautéed fish and many different variations of veal. The inside restaurant is bustling and cramped; a court-yard with tables outside is the more relaxing option.

Ristorante al 34 (Al 34) ⑧

V. Mario de' Fiori, 34	
⊘ 06 679 5091	
🚇 Metro A to Spagna	
Open: Tue–Sun 1230–1500, 1930–2300	
Reservations essential	
All credit cards accepted	
Roman-Southern Italian	
€€	

Just round the corner from the Spanish Steps, this award-winning restaurant is extremely popular with local residents. The cooking is Roman with a strong southern accent; the risotto with lobster and spaghetti *alle vongole* (clam sauce) are highly recommended, as is the candlelit, romantic atmosphere in the evening. Extremely reasonably priced for both the quality and the location.

Ristorante Nino 9

V. Borgognona, 11	
☏ 06 679 5676	
Ⓜ Metro A to Spagna	
Open: Mon–Sat 1230–1500, 1930–2300	
Reservations recommended	
All credit cards accepted	
Tuscan	
€€–€€€	

Tuscan home cooking, good wines, excellent service from waiters who seem to have been here forever, together with a liberal sprinkling of Rome's beautiful people, make this one of the area's most popular trattorias. Like all good restaurants, seasonal foods feature strongly – a cause for celebration when the first wild asparagus and truffles arrive. Specialities include cannelloni Nino and fish *alla livornese* (cooked with tomatoes and onions). Wines are reasonably priced, mainly Tuscan, with some good choices amongst the Chiantis.

Ristorante Ranieri 10

V. Mario de' Fiori, 26	
☏ 06 679 5091	
Ⓜ Metro A to Spagna	
Open: Mon–Sat 1230–1500, 1930–2300	
Reservations recommended	
All credit cards accepted	
Franco-Italian	
€€–€€€	

Opulent surroundings abound in this restaurant founded over 150 years ago by one of Queen Victoria's chefs. The extensive menu includes many variations on veal, a favourite of the Queen's, and fusion dishes such as *gnocchetti alla parigiana* (Parisian-style *gnocchi* with cheese sauce). Despite being located very close to the Spanish Steps, the prices are reasonable.

Antico Caffè Greco ⑪

V. Condotti, 86

🅜 Metro A to Spagna

Open: daily 0800–2100

No smoking area

Opposite the designer paradises of Gucci and Bulgari, this landmark, founded in 1760, still retains its faded grandeur. Once the dark red velvet upholstery and marble tables were patronised by the likes of Casanova, Wagner, Byron, Baudelaire and Shelley. Nowadays you're more likely to rub shoulders with tourists over a cup of Fortnum & Mason tea or a *granità di caffè*. Service by tail-coated waiters can be brusque and expensive, but do as the locals do and squeeze into the foyer.

Babington's Tea Rooms ⑫

Pza di Spagna, 23

Website:
www.babingtons.com

🅜 Metro A to Spagna

Open: daily 0900–2030

If you pine for boiled eggs, shepherd's pie or tea and scones, this genteel, quintessentially English establishment at the foot of the Spanish Steps overlooking Keats's house will be on your menu. It's expensive and touristy but worth a brief encounter for the curiosity value of a century-old institution.

Il Brillo Parlante ⑬

V. della Fontanella, 12

🅜 Bus to V. del Babuino

▲ Babington's Tea Rooms

Open: Mon–Sat lunch and dinner, Sun dinner only. Bar: Mon–Sat and Sun evening 1100–0200 (closed until 1930 Sun)

This atmospheric wine bar just off the Piazza del Popolo boasts a wood-burning oven. Upstairs, try its selection of good wines with cold cuts or cheese at the marble counter. Downstairs you are greeted by a vaulted cellar with a pizzeria and grill for more substantial meals.

Café Notegen  **⑭**

V. del Babuino, 159

🚇 Bus to Pza del Popolo

Open: daily 0730–0100

A slice of French café society awaits here at this traditional meeting place of artists, thespians and a good sprinkling of intellectuals. It makes a good stopping-off venue for hot and cold snacks or you can linger longer over delicious cakes and coffee.

Caffè Sogo **⑮**

V. di Ripetta, 242

🚇 Bus to V. di Ripetta

Open: daily

Not to be confused with the up-market, expensive restaurant **Sogo-Asahi**, this café has good coffee and snacks and sits alongside a Japanese grocery.

Canova **⑯**

Pza del Popolo, 16/17

🚇 Bus to Pza del Popolo

Open: daily 0800–0100

This is a great venue for catching the late afternoon sun and people watching. Traditionally always popular with a right-wing clientele – in opposition to **Rosati** (*see below*) just across the square. Nowadays their rivalry is more for first place on the piazza. As well as snacks and a restaurant, there are boutiques inside selling all kinds of gifts. An expensive haunt.

Dolci e Doni **⑰**

V. delle Carrozze, 85B

🚇 Metro A to Spagna

Open: daily 0900–2000

Good for breakfast/ brunch, light snacks and delicious cakes and chocolates. Not a late night venue, but more of a tearoom, yet it is a good find, tucked away between the Spanish Steps and Piazza del Popolo.

Enoteca Fratelli Roffi Isabelli **⑱**

V. della Croce, 76B

🚇 Metro A to Spagna

Open: daily 1130–0100 (restaurant open: 1230– 1530, 1930–2300)

An extensive choice of wines, grappa and brandy lurk in this darkly atmospheric wine bar concealed behind a discreet façade. Enjoy a glass or two at the bar whilst marvelling at the dazzling array of the wines of Italy, or try to get one of the tiny tables in the back.

Night & Day **⑲**

V. dell'Oca, 50

🚇 Bus to Pza del Popolo

Open: daily 1700–0500

One of the most popular Irish pubs around the piazza where American music is played and Guinness is on tap. Despite its name, it's more of a late-night venue – especially around 0200 – after most of the clubs close for the night.

Rosati **⑳**

Pza del Popolo, 4/5/5a

🚇 Bus to Pza del Popolo

Open: daily 0700–2330

Founded in 1922, this glamorous café used to be frequented by the likes of Pasolini, the film director, and other members of the intellectual left. People of all persuasions meet here nowadays, maybe over a *sogni romani* – the pungent house cocktail in red and yellow, the colours of the city. The interior décor is still in the orginal art-nouveau style and the location on the piazza is expensively superb.

Shops

B.B.K. ㉑

V. della Frezza, 60

🚌 Bus to V. del Corso

Open: daily except Sun and Mon am

With its abbreviation for 'Bed, Bath and Kitchen', this is a very stylish shop, excellent for browsing in. The sometimes eclectic glass and kitchenware is Italian design at its very best and you may well be tempted to take away more than you can comfortably carry!

Buccone ㉒

V. di Ripetta, 19

🚇 Metro A to Flaminio

Open: daily 0900–2030

Historic shop near to Piazza del Popolo whose well-stocked wine and spirit cellar and gastronomic delicacies are amongst the finest in Rome. There are wines from all over the world, including all of Italy's wine-growing regions. In true *enoteca* tradition, it is also an excellent place to sample a glass of wine.

C.U.C.I.N.A. ㉓

V. del Babuino, 118

🚌 Bus to Pza del Popolo

Open: Tue–Sun and Mon pm 0900–1930

Superb designer kitchenware featuring kitchen gadgets from all over the world – some high tech, others rustic. Spaghetti servers, pasta makers, coffee-pots and beautifully designed space-saving accessories all jostle for your attention. Look out also for the bottle measures for wine, which were originally designed in the 15th century.

Macelleria Mastrodi ⑮

V. di Ripetta, 36

🚌 Bus to V. del Babuino

This art-nouveau-style butcher's shop is worth a look for its sheer artistry of display – maybe even if you are vegetarian. A lamp in the shape of a winged dragon presides over the marble, wood and bronze décor fronted by a counter groaning with carnivorous delights.

Nanni ㉔

V. della Croce, 25

🚇 Metro A to Spagna

Another of the many, various, sophisticated food shops along this street. Here you may

well rub shoulders with local celebrities who come here to stock up on many specialities, including *bottarga* (Sardinian dried cod eggs, which are grated over pasta). Less exotic offerings include tangy cheeses (the vacuum-packed parmesan travels well!).

Pasta all'Uovo 25

V. della Croce, 8

🚇 Metro A to Spagna

Open: 0800–1330, 1530–1930, closed Sun and Thu pm

Superb displays of every possible type and colour of fresh and dried pasta draw you into this store. It comes in all shapes and sizes too: for a change you could ask for *favette*, put delicately, it's the shape of a hopeful bridegroom's appendage!

Tad 26

V. di San Giacomo, 5

🚇 Metro A to Flaminio

Open: Tue–Sat 1000–1900, Mon 1500–1900

In this interior design shop, old and new are beautifully combined. Again an excellent place to get ideas or to invest in a lovely fruit bowl with a cleverly incorporated drainer, or an exquisite linen tablecloth.

Picnic sites

Piazza di Spagna 27

🚇 Metro A to Spagna

▲ Pincio Gardens

The most famous piazza of all is crowded day and night; however, it makes a great place to take some time out and watch the world go by. In the middle of the square is the *Barcaccia* fountain, resembling a sinking boat. Try to find a vacant spot resting on the rim of this fountain overlooking the steps for a bird's-eye view of one of the most colourful and liveliest spots in Rome.

Pincio Gardens 28

🚇 Metro A to Flaminio

To escape the city centre, a walk up Pincio Hill behind the Piazza del Popolo will reward you with panoramic views over the city in an oasis of tranquillity.

This is one of the oldest gardens in Rome and has lovely shaded avenues of oaks, palm trees and umbrella pines. Even in ancient times there were magnificent gardens on this hill, but the existing gardens are an early 19th-century creation by Giuseppe Valadier, who was also responsible for the redesign of the Piazza del Popolo. There is an exclusive (and expensive) café-restaurant, Café Valadier, in the grounds whose customers have included Mussolini, Ghandi and King Farouk of Egypt. For the best sunset view of all go to the terrace at Piazza Napoleone to see St Peter's dome stunningly bathed in gold.

Coffee and caffè society

A shot of caffeine

Romans love their caffeine fix. No matter what time of the day or night the quick espresso is a religiously observed ritual. There are almost as many different types of coffee as there are *caffès* – from the *corretto* (the strongest black cut with a dash of grappa) at the crowded counter of a spit and sawdust bar to a *granità* (on ice) in an elegant piazza caffè. The most famous of all *caffès* is the **Sant'Eustachio** (*see page 23*) which many say serves the best coffee in the city, endorsed by all the celebrities' testimonials plastering the walls. Their speciality is the *gran caffè* which comes frothy, sweet, black and strong (if you want it unsweetened, ask for *amaro*).

If it's *caffè latte* (half milk, half coffee) or a cappuccino that you crave then you can have it *senza schiuma* (without froth) – but if it's after noon you may well get a pained look. Romans (and Italians in general) find it difficult to understand drinking coffee with milk, apart from at breakfast and during the morning. It is also more often served warm than piping hot, partly due to the fact that the coffee is prepared using water at 90°C (162°F) at great pressure, rather than at boiling, lower pressure point, and partly because it is usually drunk quickly standing up.

> **Romans (and Italians in general) find it difficult to understand drinking coffee with milk, apart from at breakfast and during the morning.**

Caffès have always played a very important role in political, literary, artistic and social life and in amorous assignations, although women were not admitted until the middle of the 17th century.

The Roman institution, **Antico Caffè Greco** (*see page 62*) was founded by a Greek in 1760 and was the regular haunt of Keats, Byron, composers such as Bizet and Liszt, and Casanova, who called it the haunt of 'a bunch of gossips, pimps, castratos and abbots'.

The sign, *torrefazione*, alongside a bar or *caffè* means

that the proprietor has a licence for coffee roasting and the delicious aroma will lead you there. **La Tazza d'Oro** bears this sign (*see page 43*) and is a great place to sample their delicious *granità di caffè* (iced coffee with whipped cream on top). But do sympathise with those who have these wonderful coffee-toasting machines but have been banned from using them by EU regulations, like the **Antico Caffè del Brasile** (*see page 12*), whose customers once included the Pope when he was still humble Cardinal Wojtyla.

In the ghetto, **Bar Da Vezio** (*V. dei Delfini, 23;* 🚌 *bus to Largo Argentina*) is not on a sunny piazza but it is very close to the Democratici di Sinistra, previously the Communist Party HQ. The walls are adorned with archives of Communist memorabilia and you can be sure of some good, thought-provoking exchanges with the owner, Vezio – a legendary figure himself.

▲ Antico Caffè Greco

One of the best spots for people watching is **Rosati** (*see page 63*) – now the preserve of the media and celebrities. Your espresso or *caffè americano* (weaker black coffee) will be very expensive but equally pleasant, especially since the piazza has become pedestrianised. **Caffè Farnese** (*see page 33*) is a good spot from which to watch the crowds bustling in from Campo de' Fiori to Piazza Farnese. The coffee (and *cornetti*) are excellent. As with everywhere else, it is much more expensive to sit down than stand at the counter with your coffee.

Ciampini al Café du Jardin (*Vle Trinità dei Monti, nr to Pza di Spagna*) has superb views from its garden setting, perfect for sipping a *macchiato* (with a drop of milk) or even a *caffè Hag* (the usual way of saying decaffeinated). At **Bar Gran Caffè dell'Opera** (*V. Torino, 140;* 🚌 *bus to V. Nazionale; open: all day, closed Mon*), located opposite the opera house of the same vintage, 1880, the walls are covered with signed photos of all the opera stars who performed there. The coffee's good too, served as elsewhere in thick porcelain cups, especially shaped to disperse the flavour evenly. But for the real, down-to-earth experience, seek out Trastevere's bohemian **Bar San Calisto** (*see page 72*) where you'll experience all of Roman *caffè* society.

Trastevere

A cross the Tiber, Rome's well-established 'bohemian' area is full of local character and is a treasure trove of good restaurants. It is also noteworthy for excellent grocery stores and characterful bars.

Villa Doria Pamphili

N

V. del Fornaci

V. S. Pancrazio

0   metres   250
0   yards   250

TRASTEVERE
Restaurants

Alberto Ciarla ❶

Pza di San Cosimato, 40

✆ 06 581 8668

🚍 Bus to Vle di Trastevere

Open: Mon–Sat 2000–2400

Reservations essential

All credit cards accepted

Seafood

€€€

The full-sized diver dummy at the entrance sets the scene for exquisite seafood dining. In elegantly dramatic décor that blends red and black with a sea theme, the dishes are spectacular in creativity and freshness of ingredients. The raw and smoked fish is excellent, as is the seafood salad, perhaps followed by a *secondo* of *filetto di spigola alle erbe* (sea bass). As you would expect from the president of the Italian sommeliers, Alberto Ciarla has an exceptional wine list. Expensive, sophisticated dining.

Antico Arco ❷

Pzle Aurelio, 7

✆ 06 581 5274

🚍 Bus to V. Carini

Open: Mon–Sat 2000–2400

Reservations essential

All credit cards accepted

Roman-Italian

€€–€€€

Patrizia, Maurizio and Domenico moved to this elegant old restaurant from their former home, **Il Bacaro** (*see page 39*) in 1996 and provide some of the best-value gourmet dining in Rome. Good pasta dishes, sea bass and the excellent *bourguignonne di fletto all'aceto*

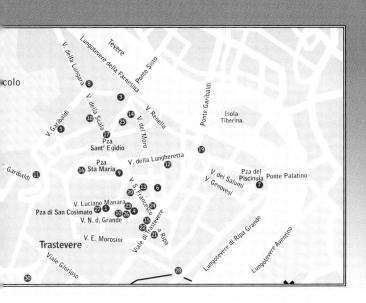

balsamico tradizione di Modena (fillet beef bourguignonne with balsamic vinegar) are especially recommended.

Checco er Carrettiere ❸

V. Benedetta, 10

✆ 06 580 0985

🚌 Bus to Vle di Trastevere

Open: lunch and dinner, closed Sun evening

Reservations recommended

All credit cards accepted

Roman cuisine

€€–€€€

This well-established Trastevere monument to traditional cooking has been popular for the last forty years. Resisting

▲ Alberto Ciarla at his restaurant

any concessions to fusion-style cuisine, here you will find good seafood and homemade Roman specialities in typical surroundings. A pleasant garden offers al fresco dining.

Corsetti-II Galeone ❹

Pza di San Cosimato, 27

✆ 06 580 9009

🚍 Bus to Vle di Trastevere

Open: daily 1200–1530, 2000–2400, closed Wed lunch

Reservations recommended

All credit cards accepted

Roman-Seafood

●●●

Established in 1921, this old favourite has pole position on Trastevere's bustling piazza. As the name suggests, the dining room on the first floor is like a galleon, full of ships' lanterns and wood panelling with a menu devoted to seafood, whilst the ground floor serves good traditional Roman fare. Touristy and not cheap, but the location with pavement tables is hard to beat.

Da Lucia ❺

Vicolo del Mattonato, 2

✆ 06 580 3601

🚍 Bus to Vle di Trastevere

Open: Tue–Sun 1230–1530, 1930–2300

Reservations recommended

No credit cards accepted

Roman cooking

●

One of Rome's oldest trattorias where reliable

dishes such as *baccalà* and *pollo con peperoni* (chicken with peppers) feature. Not quite right for the special night out, but cheapness, crowds and cheerfulness are the winning ingredients: the outdoor tables are especially attractive in summer.

Paris ❻

Pza di San Calisto, 7A

✆ 06 581 5378

🚍 Bus to Vle di Trastevere

Open: 1200–1500, 1830–2300, closed Sun evening and Mon

Reservations essential

All credit cards accepted

Roman-Jewish cuisine

●●–●●●

A Trastevere institution which has been around for a century or more. Traditional dishes such as *trippa alla romana* and zucchini flowers stuffed with anchovies and mozzarella are favourite dishes, alongside good fresh fish and excellent *fritto misto vegetale* (fresh fried vegetables). A highly convivial atmosphere, coupled with fine wines, complete this very popular restaurant's appeal.

Peccati di Gola ❼

Pza dei Ponziani, 7A

✆ 06 581 4529

🚍 Bus to Lungotevere degli Anguillara

Open: Tue–Sun 1300–1500, 2000–2400

Reservations recommended

All credit cards accepted

Seafood

●●●

The name translated as 'the sins of gluttony' is apt for this elegant, typically Roman restaurant devoted to the pleasures of the table. Mostly classical in style, but there is a Calabrian influence, which gives robust flavours to the predominantly fish dishes. The tables outside are extremely popular during the summer.

Romolo (nel Giardino della Fornarina) ❽

V. di Porta Settimania, 8

✆ 06 581 8284

🚍 Bus to Vle di Trastevere

Open: Tue–Sun 1300–1500, 1930–2400

Reservations recommended

All credit cards accepted

Roman cuisine

●●–●●●

The former home of Raphael's model and mistress, Margherita, known as *La Fornarina* (the baker's girl). Now a very popular restaurant and excellent location for a leisurely lunch in the walled courtyard, or candlelit dinner to the accompaniment of a wistful guitar. The traditional Roman fare includes very good fresh pasta with radish or artichoke sauce and the speciality, mozzarella *alla Fornarina*.

Sabatini ❾

Pza Sta Maria in Trastevere, 13

✆ 06 581 2026

🚍 Bus to Vle di Trastevere

Open: daily 1200–1500, 2000–2400

Reservations recommended

All credit cards accepted

Roman-Seafood

€€€

Once a favourite of the late Fellini, this well sought-after dining spot has lost none of its appeal and, even if you have a reservation, you sometimes have to wait. The selection of *antipasti* is legendary in the area and the spaghetti with seafood and superb chicken are especially recommended. There is a branch of the restaurant in Tokyo, so you might get a trainee Japanese waiter! The house wines of Frascati and Chianti served in pitchers are good value, otherwise you may well be offered very expensive alternatives.

Da Vittorio ⑩

V. di San Cosimato, 14A

✆ 06 580 0353

🚌 Bus to Vle di Trastevere

Open: Mon–Sat 1830–2400

Reservations not allowed

No credit cards accepted

Pizza/pasta

€

Delicious pizza *neapolitana*, the soft thick variety loaded with fresh tomatoes and anchovies, hints at the Neapolitan influence here in this bustling pizzeria. The walls are lined with pin-ups from the region and shelves of wine bottles and hanging objects, all vying for space. Pasta also features along with some salads and *antipasti*, but try the pizza 'Enzo', named after patron Enzo Martino, for the full flavour of Napoli. Tables outside are very popular with the young set.

TRASTEVERE
Bars, cafés and pubs

Baretti ⑪

V. Garibaldi, 27

🚌 Bus to Lungotevere
Sanzio

Open: 0800–2300, closed
Sun

Enjoy superb views
from this café over the
rooftops of Trastevere
and over the Janiculum
Hill. A terrace table is
the ideal place to enjoy
these over a coffee or
drink, whilst inside a
juke box of 1960s
vintage quietly plays
hits of the old days.

Bar Gianicolo ②

Pzle Aurelia, 5

🚌 Bus to V. Carini

Open: Tue–Sun 0600–0300

On the site of Garibaldi's
doomed battle with the
French, this tiny atmos-
pheric bar is also a
stone's throw from the
American Academy. It's
a good spot for coffee
and a *cornetto* or freshly
squeezed lemon, carrot
or apple juice. Other
snacks include exotic
sandwiches or you can
just enjoy a drink at one
of the outside tables.

Bar San Calisto
(also known as
Marcello's) ⑫

Pza di San Calisto

🚌 Bus to V. Trastevere

Open: Mon–Sat 0530–0200

Spit and sawdusty,
seedy even, but this is
where the locals hang
out over a glass of
prosecco (sparkling
white wine) or one of
Marcello's homemade
delicious ice creams.
If you prefer not to
stand at the counter,
the outside tables
overlooking the square
give a window on the
real Trastevere world
with plenty of colour-
ful (sometimes eclectic)
characters, so you
may want to linger
awhile!

Bibli ⑬

V. dei Fienaroli, 28

Website: *www.bibli.it*

🚌 Bus to Pza Sonnino

Open: Tue–Sun and Mon
evening 1100–2400

This bookshop-café-
cinema-tearoom and
music venue is a great
place for Sunday
brunch, which is now
becoming a popular
Roman custom.
There are around
30,000 publications to
browse over, some of
which are in English,
and it also serves
sandwiches and salads.
If you are getting
withdrawal symptoms
you can log on to
the internet, as you
sip your espresso and
chat to friends.

Enoteca Ferrara ⑭

V. del Moro, 1A

🚌 Bus/tram to Vle
Trastevere

Open: 2030–0200, closed
Tue and Sun in summer

You'll find a well-
stocked cellar in this big
wine bar, which unlike
many other *enoteche*
stays open late.
Excellent homemade
soups, cheese and salad
complement an exten-
sive list of over 200
wines. On balmy
evenings head into an
attractive, quiet garden
to relax in a calm and
peaceful oasis in the
heart of Trastevere.

Frontoni
(dal 1921) ⑮

Vle di Trastevere, 52

🚌 Bus to V. Trastevere

Open: daily 0730–0100

A pristine bar-café
serving a range of
snacks where the
speciality is white pizza
with a choice of 60
different fillings,
including delicious
sausage, ham and
onion. With excellent,
friendly service, this is a
very popular takeaway
place for local workers,
especially at lunchtime.

Di Marzio ⑯

Pza Sta Maria in Trastevere,
15

This atmospheric piazza demands to be sat in and lingered over with a long, cool drink. Situated right opposite the church of Santa Maria, this café-bar has good, albeit expensive, drinks and snacks but the most important part of the experience is – location, location, location.

Ombre Rosse **⑰**

Pza Sant'Egidio, 12

⊙ Bus to Pza Sonnino

Open: Mon–Sat and Sun
evening 0700–0200

The Ombre Rossa is a mixture of a *birreria* and a wine bar which sells wine by the glass, many different types of beer and a huge selection of whiskies. As usual, there are tasty accompanying light snacks in this friendly hostelry in a lovely Trastevere piazza.

La Scala **⑱**

V. della Scala, 4

⊙ Bus to Vle di Trastevere

Open: daily 1600–0200

This big, busy and crowded hostelry is perhaps the most popular of all the *birrerie* in Trastevere. Music, cheap beer, cocktails, wine by the glass and pub grub are all on offer. If it's too dark and smoky inside, join the late-night revellers spilling out on to the tables on the Via della Scala.

Trastè **⑲**

V. della Lungheretta, 76

⊙ Bus to Vle Trastevere

Open: daily 1700–0130

More for the serene than as a place for heavy late-night drinking, you can try interesting teas and cakes, which are quite a rarity in Trastevere.

▲ Santa Maria

TRASTEVERE
Shops, markets and picnic sites

Shops

AZI 20

V. San Francesco a Ripa, 170

🚌 Bus to V. Trastevere

Open: 0930–1330, 1600–2000, closed Sun am

You'll see Italian design at its best in this treasure trove of things for the home where even the dustbins are stylish! The terracotta and glass goods are especially attractive and not extortionately priced either.

Il Canestro 21

V. San Francesco a Ripa, 106

🚌 Bus to V. Trastevere

Open: Tue–Sat 0900–2000, Mon 1200–2000

One of the pioneers of macrobiotic foods and still amongst the city's best-stocked retailers of organic produce, Il Canestro also has courses on alternative medicine and nutrition. (The main branch is at *V. Luca della Robbia, 12 – see page 14.*)

La Casa del Tramezzino 22

Vle di Trastevere, 1

🚌 Bus to Vle Trastevere

Open: daily 0700–0200

A sandwich bar with a difference: it boasts the widest choice in Rome with everything from cheese and tomato to caviar. Incidentally, the mouthful, '*tramezzino*' (sandwich) was coined by Mussolini when he decreed that foreign words should be replaced with home-grown Italian ones.

Drogheria Innocenzi 23

Pza di San Cosimato, 66

🚌 Bus to V. Trastevere

Open: 0700–1330, 1630–1930, closed Sun and Thu pm

An unprepossessing doorway leads into an Aladdin's cave of pasta, polenta, herbs, rice and flour by the sack full, bottles of every shape and size and any comestible you care to mention. Established in 1884, people travel here literally from far and wide to stock up and learn from owner, Sandro, about all the regional specialities and products, from abroad too, which you would find difficult to find elsewhere in the city. The San Cosimato door is often closed, so try the side entrance at Via Natale del Grande, 31.

Fratelli Longhi 24

V. San Francesco a Ripa, 19

🚌 Bus to V. Trastevere

Open: daily except Thu pm and Jewish holidays

The Fratelli brothers have mouth-watering temptations all jumbled into this little delicatessen. Specialities include cold meats and cheese and kosher delicacies, reflecting the history of Trastevere.

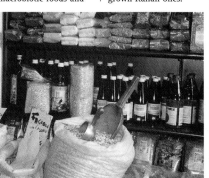

▲ Drogheria Innocenzi

Lattonieri 25

Pza de'Renzi, 22 (off the northern end of Vle di Trastevere)

🚌 Bus to Lungotevere Sanzio

Open: Mon–Sat and Sun pm

Tinplate coffee-pots, oil and vinegar servers, lanterns and all kinds of other utensils are lovingly crafted by two brothers. As they are made of tin, they are not especially heavy and you can have your own special souvenir made to order too.

Pizza Roma 26

Pza di San Cosimato, 48–9

✆ 06 581 3541

🚌 Bus to V. Trastevere

Open: daily

Thirty-seven types of pizza feature on the takeaway menu here, not counting the custom-made ones, plus chips (*crocchette di papate*), fried courgette flowers and the ubiquitous *filletti di baccalà*. A phone-out service is available too.

Markets

Piazza di San Cosimato 27

🚌 Bus to V. Trastevere

Open: Mon–Sat 0700–1300

The little square overflows with food vendors and their stalls every morning. It's always touristy with many more people intent on photographic opportunities than buying produce, but lively,

▲ Cheese stall

bustling and full of neighbourhood charm nonetheless.

Porta Portese 28

V. Portese

🚌 Bus to Ponte Sublicio

Open: Sun only, 0500–1400

This, the largest flea market in Europe, is full of entertaining junk and even the occasional antique or designer item. Although not a food market, you may be able to pick up bargain tableware – or even the contessa's high table cast-offs. Go early, before 1000 if you can, and be especially wary of pickpockets here – it's often said that if your valuables are stolen they always end up at Porta Portese – and with reason!

Picnic sites

Janiculum (Il Gianicolo) 29

🚌 Bus 870 from Trastevere

From the Janiculum hill you get the best views

of all of the city – on a clear day to the mountains beyond – and a climb up to the park, **Passeggiata del Gianocolo**, will reward you with its pleasant cool and shaded gardens. It is especially popular with families at the weekends, with amusements such as Punch and Judy and merry-go-rounds, and several refreshment kiosks to bolster your picnic.

Sciarra Villa Park 30

V. Calandrelli, 35

🚌 Bus to V. Dandolo

Open: 0900–sunset

You get marvellous views over the city from this small, lovely park. In Roman times it was the site of a nymph's sanctuary and the paths are full of statues, fountains and Romantic follies. It is especially picturesque in springtime with the cherry blossom and wisteria in bloom.

Wine and enoteche

In vino veritas!

Frascati is just 21 kilometres outside Rome, home to the vineyards which produce one of Italy's best-known white wines. Romans normally drink white wine, and the house wine (*vino della casa* or *vino locale*) served in your trattoria is most likely to be one from the Castelli Romani area of which Frascati is part. Also worth trying is Est!Est!Est! from surrounding Lazio: a well-priced dry white, great for drinking chilled on a hot summer's day. However, although drinkable and modestly priced, these are not wines of great character and, generally, those produced in the region are regarded as inferior to Italian wine as a whole. For a few lire more you could order a **Frascati Superiore**, **Velletri**, **Marino** or **Colli Albani** – all of which are made from the same Trebbiano

grape variety, sometimes with a hint of Malvasia grapes for flavour and bouquet.

The main classification of wine, clearly printed on the label, is DOC (*denominazione di origine controllata*) where, although not a guarantee of high quality, the wine comes from the region and is made from designated grape varieties. DOCG (*denominazione di origine controllata e garantita*) is quality led, has been tested by government inspectors and is reserved only for the top wines. Whatever your choice, the golden rule with most Italian white wine is that it should be drunk within a year of bottling and, of course, should be served cold – *un secchiello di ghiaccio* (an ice bucket) is a useful phrase! There is also a big trend towards the young sparkling white wines as an *aperitivo*: **Prosecco**, **Vignanello**, **Galestro Capsula Viola** and **Glicine** are favourites, all of which should be drunk as young as possible.

Of the reds, although some are made locally, most of the bottled red wine that you find in Rome comes from other regions of Italy, mostly from Tuscany and Chianti. Rattan-covered flasks on the *o sole mio* theme are definitely to

▲ Wine dispenser at Est!Est!Est!

be avoided! Try instead a **Chianti Classico Riserva** – stronger and more mature than a normal *classico*, or treat yourself to a heavenly **Barolo** from Piedmont. The local red served up tends to be from the Abruzzi region east of Rome: **Montepulciano d'Abruzzo** is a reliable, good value, juicy wine, but the variety produced in very small quantities by **Edoardo Valentini** is sublime – and expensive.

To sample some of these wines, *enoteche* (wine bars) are extremely popular and keep popping up all over the city. Rome's first modern(ish) wine bar, founded in 1968, is the **Cul de Sac** near Piazza Navona (*see page 22*) which offers a great selection of wines and mostly cold foods. The **Antica Enoteca di Via della Croce** (*V. della Croce;* ⊛ *metro to Spagna; open: daily 1115–0100; all credit cards accepted*), founded in 1842, was a favourite haunt of artists living in Via Margutta. They have an interesting selection of wines by the glass and a cold buffet.

In the *centro stórico*, **La Bottega del Vino da Anacleto Bleve** (*see page 32*) has 2 000 different carefully selected wines in the shop with different tastings each week and excellent food. Their speciality is advice and hospitality. At the dark, small and very atmospheric **Enoteca Fratelli Roffi Isabelli** (*see page 77*) the speciality is Italian wines, brandies and grappa (a potent

▲ Il Simposio

liquor made from grapes). Down the road at the Forum end is **Cavour 313** (*see page 12*) which has an excellent choice of wines and a good selection of hot and cold snacks. **La Vineria** (*see page 33*) is a popular spot right on the Campo de' Fiori which also sells very reasonably priced wine by the glass at the bar. Around Piazza Navona **L'Angolo Divino** (*V. dei Balestrari, 12;* ⊛ *bus to Largo Argentina; open: daily*) has themed wine-tasting evenings throughout the year amongst charming wooden beams and terracotta floors.

The golden rule with most Italian white wine is that it should be drunk within a year of bottling and, of course, should be served cold.

For a true Bacchanalian experience, **Il Simposio di Piero Costantini** (*see page 83*) is the ultimate in grape and vine motif decoration and is especially popular with Romans who favour it as much for the food as the wine. **Trimani Wine Bar** (*see page 53*) is an offshoot of Rome's oldest and perhaps best wine shop, **Trimani Enoteca** (*see page 55*). Extremely popular, it serves good quality food too and, as you would expect, has a superb choice of Italian regional wines.

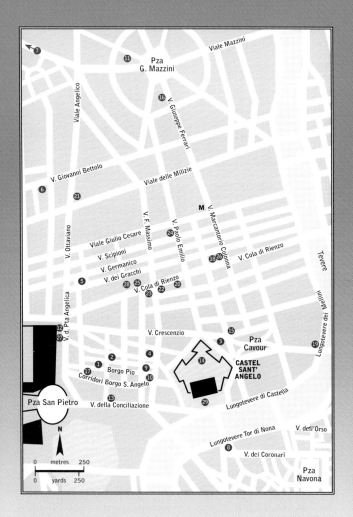

Vatican and Prati

A way from the touristy establishments immediately surrounding St Peter's and the Castel Sant'Angelo, there are good local restaurants, some definitely worthy of a special trip. The area also boasts one of the highest concentrations of delicatessens in a single street.

VATICAN AND PRATI
Restaurants

Arlù ❶

Borgo Pio, 135

✆ 06 686 8936

🚍 Bus to V. di Porta Castello

Open: Mon–Sat 1200–1500, 2000–2300

Reservations recommended

All credit cards accepted

Creative cuisine

€€

In the maze of medieval streets known as the Borgo, this atmospheric little restaurant is both intimate and elegant – the perfect setting for a romantic, candlelit dinner. The food is creative and sophisticated with a skilful blend of flavours – try the *tonnarelli* with orange sauce.

Da Benito e Gilberto al Falco ❷

V. del Falco, 19

✆ 06 686 7769

🚍 Bus to V. Crescenzio

Open: Tue–Sat 1300–1530, 1930–2330

Reservations essential

All credit cards accepted

Seafood

€€

Tucked away in the Borgo area, this small, family-run restaurant is always busy. Photographs of the latter-day high society set adorn the walls but the present-day stars come here too, including the likes of Benardo Bernini of *La Vita è Bella* fame. As well as star gazing, foodies are treated to superb fresh fish, (almost) live crustaceans, good pasta and richly garnished *secondi*.

Da Cesare ❸

V. Crescenzio, 13

✆ 06 686 1227

🚍 Bus to Pza Cavour

Open: Tue–Sat lunch and dinner, Sun lunch

Reservations unnecessary

All credit cards accepted

Trattoria-Pizzeria

€–€€

Traditional trattoria with a pleasant, well-established ambience. Specialities include hearty soups, truffles, *porcini* mushrooms and game, when in season.

▲ The Vatican

It also features Tuscan variations and delicious fresh fish.

Les Étoiles ④

Hotel Atlante Star
V. dei Bastioni, 1/V. Vitelleschi, 34
✆ 06 687 3233
Website: *www.atlantehotels.com*
🚍 Bus to V. di Porta Castello
Open: daily 1230–1430, 1930–2230
Reservations recommended
All credit cards accepted
Classic cuisine
€€€

This rooftop restaurant accessed by a lift enjoys one of the most stunning views of Rome with the dome of St Peter's seemingly at arm's length. Dining here will cost you the proverbial arm and leg, but the cuisine and service are usually sound. The menu changes daily, but specialities include snails with truffles and pecorino cheese, and quail's eggs with rocket and mustard dressing.

Il Matriciano ⑤

V. dei Gracchi, 55
✆ 06 321 2327
Ⓜ Metro A to Ottaviano
Open: daily 1230–1500, 2000–2400
Reservations recommended
All credit cards accepted
Roman cuisine
€€

Conveniently located for St Peter's, you may well find the true meaning of eating becoming a religion here. This busy, family-run restaurant has a devoted following from cardinals to film makers, including director Anthony Minghella who spent many 'unforgettable hours' here while filming *The Talented Mr. Ripley*. The *abbacchio* (lamb), ravioli *di ricotta, stracetti de pezza* (shredded beef and arugula) are all consumed with great gusto, attended by the jovial gravity of ancient waiters. The shady outside tables are extremely popular on hot days and nights where a wandering minstrel may well try to serenade you.

Osteria dell'Angelo ⑥

V. Giovanni Bettolo, 24
✆ 06 372 9470
Ⓜ Metro A to Ottaviano
Open: Mon–Fri and Sat evening 1230–1430, 2000–2400
Reservations essential
No credit cards accepted
Roman cuisine
€

A set price, excellent value menu in the evening could include delicious skate soup (*minestra di arzilla*), wild-boar sausage or many other tasty traditional dishes; wine is included too. The walls of this very popular, typical *osteria* are plastered with photos of boxers and rugby players, in keeping with Angelo's sporting past. The lunchtime menu is à la carte and not as busy as the evening when reservations are essential.

La Pergola dell'Hotel Hilton ⑦

V. Cadlolo, 101
✆ 06 3509 2211
🚍 Bus to Pza Medaglia d'Oro
Open: Tue–Sat 1930–2345
Reservations essential
All credit cards accepted
Mediterranean haute cuisine
€€€

Young German chef Heinz Beck has brought a huge amount of accolades to this elegant rooftop restaurant, including a coveted Michelin star and a 'Grande' rating from the *Espresso Guide*, naming it one of the best restaurants in the whole of Italy. Dishes such as *carpaccio di scampi con caviale* (scampi with caviar) are sublime, as is the ravioli *di verdura con frutti di mare*. In fact Beck seems to have the Midas touch with all his dishes, not least the superb puddings: *mousse al caffè 'la Pergola'* is the closest possible thing to a chocoholic's heaven. Here, from Monte Mario, the views are heavenly, the service impeccable and the bill breathtaking.

Le Streghe 8

Vicolo del Curato, 13

✆ 06 686 1381

Bus to V. di Porta Castello

Open: Mon–Sat, closed Sun

Reservations recommended

All credit cards accepted

Creative cuisine

€€

Just over the river next to the bridge to St Peter's, this romantic little restaurant started life as a distraction for three bored wives, known affectionately as the three 'witches' (*streghe*). Now their creativity in the kitchen has made this eatery famous and is very busy in the evenings, especially with local aristocratic families and a few celebrities. The spaghetti with truffles and broccoli is especially tasty, the fresh fruit sorbets exceptional and the candlelit atmosphere is made even more mellow by the strains of a classical guitarist.

Taverna Angelica 9

Pza delle Vaschette, 14A

✆ 06 687 4514

Bus to V. della Conciliazione

Open: Tue–Sat and Mon evening 1230–1430, 1930–2400

Reservations recommended

American Express Mastercard Visa Eurocheque

Creative cuisine

€€€

Elegant, romantic restaurant run by a young and enthusiastic team in the labyrinth of lanes in front of St Peter's known as the Borgo area. A constantly changing menu reflects the seasons with a strong emphasis on seafood and some inventive combinations such as balsamic vinegared chicken in a *jus* of squid ink.

Tre Pupazzi 10

V. dei tre Pupazzi, 1/Borgo Pio

✆ 06 686 8371

Bus to V. di Porta Castello

Open: Mon–Sat lunch and dinner (late)

Reservations unnecessary

American Express Visa Mastercard

Roman–Italian

€

Founded in 1625, this trattoria takes its name not from 'three puppets' (fortunately) but the barely distinguishable stone figures on an old sarcophagus near the Vatican. The food is tasty, with standard fare including excellent fish, pasta dishes, *abbacchio* and good pizzas at lunch as well as dinner.

▲ The Vatican State

VATICAN AND PRATI
Bars, cafés and pubs

▲ Castel Sant'Angelo

Antonini ⑪

V. Sabotino, 21–9

🚌 Bus to Pza Mazzini

Open: daily 0700–2100

One of Rome's very best *pasticcerie* which also serves delicious savouries, such as *tartine* topped with pâté or caviar. Indulge yourself here amidst the smart set and watch the well-heeled buy their cakes for a dinner party or celebration.

Bar Santa Anna ⑫

V. Sta Anna, 18

🚇 Metro A Ottaviano

Open: daily

Tucked away one block north of St Peter's, this is a good spot for excellent sandwiches and bar snacks, and prices are reasonable even if you sit down rather than prop up the bar.

Caffè San Pietro ⑬

V. della Conciliazione, 40

🚇 Metro A to Ottaviano

Open: Tue–Sun

Notorious as the place where Ali Agca had his coffee before attempting to assassinate Pope John Paul II in St Peter's Square. However, it is a good spot for a light lunch or drink, well situated for the Vatican.

Castel Sant' Angelo ⑭

Lungotevere Castello, 50

🚌 Bus to V. Tiboniano

Open: daily 0900–1900, closed second and fourth Tue of the month

Connected to the Vatican by a long corridor, this fortress is one of Rome's top attractions. A wonderful place to admire the beautiful view from the terrace, but don't be tempted to re-enact poor Tosca's fate when, in the last scene of Puccini's opera, she jumped to her death from here. Instead, have a coffee or light lunch in one of the rampart towers.

Enoteca Costantini (Il Simposio di Piero Costantini) ⑮

Pza Cavour, 16

✆ 06 321 3210

🚌 Bus to Pza Cavour

Open: Mon–Fri, Sat and Sun evenings 1130–1500, 1830–0100

€€€

From the moment you walk through the wrought-iron doors encrusted with vine and grapes, you know that you have entered a Bacchanalian paradise. The cellars hold over 4 000 bottles of wine, whilst on the ground floor you can sample a glass or two with a selection of snacks and cheeses. Behind heavy velvet curtains lies the restaurant which offers excellent full meals.

Faggiani ⑯

V. Giuseppe Ferrari, 23/5

🚇 Metro A to Lepanto

Open: daily 0730–2100

Enjoy a cappuccino and *cornetto* in this family bar, attached to another of the best *pasticcerie* in

Rome. Or simply relax over a drink and sample the delicious rice confection *budino di riso*, probably the best Rome has to offer.

Al Mio Caffè ⑰

Pza Città Leonina, 7

🚇 Metro A to Ottaviano

Open: daily 0530–1930

Just a stone's throw from St Peter's, try perhaps a delicious *spremuta di limone*, *arancia* or *pompelino* (freshly squeezed lemon, orange or grapefruit juice). Light snacks include fresh rolls and sandwiches.

Pellachia ⑱

V. Cola di Rienzo, 103

🚌 Bus to V. Cola di Rienzo

Open: Tue–Sun 0630–1300

A good place to recover from retail therapy on Prati's busiest shopping street. Enjoy a drink at this popular bar or indulge in some of the best ice creams north of the Tiber.

Ruschena ⑲

Lungotevere dei Mellini, 1

🚌 Bus to V. Tomacelli

Open: daily except Mon

This old-fashioned patisserie on the banks of the Tiber commands wonderful views over the domes of Rome. Popular with ladies of a certain age as well as the young and beautiful who come to indulge in the mouth-watering cakes – the millefeuille is especially delicious.

VATICAN AND PRATI
Shops, markets and picnic sites

Shops

Castroni ⑳

V. Cola di Rienzo, 196

🅜 Metro A to Ottaviano

Open: Mon–Sat 0800–2000

The delicious aroma of coffee greets you on entering this famous shop, resembling a miniature version of Fortnum & Mason. In this heavenly scented gastronomic paradise all kinds of teas (including Earl Grey), preserves, dried mushrooms, darkest and richest chocolate, and regional specialities mingle with international food staples such as Marmite. You can also sample the coffee and delicious cakes at the bar.

G Chirico (Tortellini) ㉓

V. Cola di Rienzo, 211

🅜 Metro A to Ottaviano

Open: Mon–Sat 0800–2000

Pasta, pasta – in all shapes, sizes and colours. Whether it's fresh or the dried variety, you will find over 50 different kinds to choose from here in this tiny, family-run shop. You can also invest in the most delicious and greenest extra virgin olive oil and little bottles of exquisite and expensive truffle oil – a little goes a long way.

Emporium Naturae ㉑

Vle Angelico, 2

🅜 Metro A to Ottaviano

Open: Mon–Sat

As its name suggests, this is a supermarket devoted to healthfood – one of a very rare breed as Rome's shops tend to be of the small, grocery variety whilst the supermarkets are relegated to the outskirts. Here you

will find a wide range of organic and health foods both packaged and fresh.

Franchi (Benedetto Franchi)  22

V. Cola di Rienzo, 200/204
Website: www.franchi.it
Metro A to Ottaviano
Open: daily 0815–2100

The main shopping street in the area is a gourmet's paradise and Franchi is one of the best *salumeria* and *rosticceria* in town. You can purchase everything, from pâté *de foie gras*, terrines, salamis, cheese and wine to takeaway pizzas and sumptuous delicacies for a picnic.

G Giuliani 24

V. Paolo Emilio, 67
Metro A to Ottaviano
Open: daily 0830–2000, Sun 0900–1300

Confectioner Giuliani has been making the most delicious *marrons glacés* for more than 45 years, which is why so many Italians travel from afar to buy them by the kilo. Mouth-wateringly delicious, perhaps the naughty but nice treat you need after all that sightseeing at the Vatican.

Habitat 25

V. Cola di Rienzo, 197
Metro A to Ottaviano
Open: Mon–Sat

Perhaps more for window-shopping than buying, but an excellent shop for inspiration for the kitchen and table back home. Good home wares including kitchen utensils, glassware, rugs, furniture and haberdashery are all distinctively Italian-styled.

New Old 26

V. Marcantonio Colonna, 12
Metro A to Lepanto
Open: Tue–Sat 0930–1330, 1600–2000, Mon 1600–2000

A veritable treasure trove of designer gadgets, from fondue dishes to coffee-pots, saucepans, skillets, silver trays and even plastic tableware. All this is on offer alongside more traditional furniture and housewares – but the underlying theme here is style.

Pizzeria Il Migliore 27

V. Santa Anna
Metro A to Ottaviano
Open: 0900–2100, closed Sun

Just down from the **Bar Santa Anna** (*see page 83*) this pizza stand offers a huge and delicious variety of pizza *a taglio* (by the slice) at very reasonable prices per 100 grammes (*etto*).

Markets

Piazza dell'Unità 28

Metro A to Ottaviano
Open: Mon–Fri 0800–2000, Sat 0800–1400

Just off the Via Cola di Rienzo, this covered market is always popular for its fresh produce at reasonable prices. Ideal for stocking up for a good picnic.

Picnic sites

Castel Sant'Angelo Park 29

Bus to V. Crescenzio

Don't let the fact that this was the place where poor Tosca fell to her death interfere with your enjoyment – this is a little oasis of greenery.

Glorious gelato

A riot of taste and colour

A *gelato* with your *passeggiata* or sitting in a fountain-splashed piazza, or whenever the mood takes you, is one of the great pleasures of Rome. Every bar worth your lire will have its own homemade version and, in the ice cream parlours (*gelaterie*) everything from frozen *tiramisù*, pistachio and even After Eight variations are on offer. '*Produzione artigianale*' (homemade ice cream) is the sign to seek out, although sometimes the acid bright colours may make you question their provenance; however, they are usually still scrumptious. If the *gelato* is kept in aluminium containers inside the freezer, it usually means that it has, indeed, been made on the premises, whilst exert a little more caution if it is served out of plastic ones. It is also said that the real artistes of the *gelato* world hide their delicious delights

away from general view behind the counter.

Once you start to scrape the icy surface, though, there are many different types: from *frutta* and *crema* – the classics – to *sorbetto* (sorbet) and the slightly rougher cut version, *granità*, then *semifreddo* (resembling half-frozen sponge pudding in consistency, rather like *tiramisù*). Then there is *grattachecca*, the celebrated water ice, so wonderfully cooling in the Roman summer, with the ice lovingly and painstakingly hand-grated with flavoured juice (or syrup) drizzled over the top. Just around the corner from the Pantheon, **La Cremeria Monforte** (*V. della Rotonda, 22;* ◉ *bus to Largo Argentina; closed Mon*) has yet another variation – the *cremolati*. These fruity slushes, a sort of hybrid of all the above, also come in delicious chocolatey flavours with huge chunks of chocolate in them. The highlight of the year is late July or early August when there is a *gelato* guzzling competition.

If you just want to grab a *gelato* on the move, a lot of the kiosks tend to be on the corner (*angolo*) of two streets. Their opening times are more erratic than the smart full-blown ice cream parlours as they are dependent on the weather and seasons. The **Sora Mirella** kiosk in Trastevere (*Lungotevere degli Anguillara, angolo Ponte Cestio;*

usually open: daily until 0300) is run by Mirella, the self-styled queen (*regina*) of *grattachecca* (water ices). Her sons use iron gloves to grate the ice by hand – a labour of love – but the results are fit for a queen or king!

Gelateria della Palma (*see page 43*) is an experience more than just an ice cream parlour. With over 100 *gelati* flavours, frozen yoghurts and mousses, many agree that for this kind of oral delight, nowadays this is Rome's best. **Giolitti** (*see page 43*) with its Louis XVI-style tearooms, once the haunt of writers and artists, is, others say, still the best for ice creams and sorbets. Not to be confused with its better-known namesake, **Giolitti a Testaccio** (*see page 14*), this ever-popular institution has delicious *gelati* and *granite* and a sublime *cappuccino freddo*.

Behind the Trevi Fountain, at **San Crespino** (*V. della Panetteria, 42; closed Tue*) you will find the *gelato* viewed as an art form: both preparation and recipes are closely-guarded secrets of the brothers Pasquale and Giuseppe. Flavours are distinctively seasonal and according to the best possible fresh produce available – the summer raspberry (*lampone*) is simply fantastic. Unusual scrumptious flavours include nougat and caramel, ginger and cinnamon.

At **Alberto Pica** (*see page 32*) prizes for excellence adorn the

walls where 50 different flavours are on offer, from the savoury, shrimp or gorgonzola to Amalfi lemon or rice. **Fiocco di Neve** (*see page 45*) has crunchy rice added to many of the flavours, including delicious chestnut. In Trastevere, **La Fontana della Salute** (*V. Cardinal Marmaggi, 2–6*) has very generous portions whilst the **Bar San Calisto** (*see page 72*) has, some say, the best chocolate ice in the whole of Rome made by the owner Marcello himself. But for the ultimate in 'choco-*gelato*' delight the **Café Tre Scalini** (*see page 23*) is without equal. The chocolate *tartufo* is the ice cream equivalent of the truffle: gourmet, expensive and glorious!

The celebrated water ice, so wonderfully cooling in the Roman summer, with the ice lovingly and painstakingly hand-grated with flavoured juice drizzled over the top.

Food etiquette and culture

The choice of restaurants can be bewildering, but every taste and dining experience is catered for in this city. If you venture just a few streets away from a famous piazza and ancient monument and don't allow yourself to be put off by a dingy exterior, so often you will find a culinary paradise behind that paint-flaked doorway: take your lead from the locals!

CHOOSING AN EATERY

The *tavola calda* ('hot table'), which often serves cold food as well, has buffet-style pasta, vegetable dishes and meat, ideal for lunchtimes. *Rosticcerie* specialise in cooked meats but usually have a large selection of takeaway food for a picnic. There is a wide choice of *alimentari* (delicatessens) and *pizzerie* where you can buy pizza *a taglio* (by the slice). The *osteria* usually offers a small selection of dishes, in sometimes cramped and less than luxurious surroundings, complete with paper tablecloths and unflattering lighting – but *osterias* are often amongst the

best and cheapest eateries in town. *Trattorie* are a cheaper version of a restaurant, usually family-run with good home cooking. There is an unwritten rule that the worse the murals are on the wall, the better the food! Confusingly, many establishments which are really *trattorie* call themselves restaurants and vice versa, perhaps part of the trend towards *cucina povera* (down-to-earth 'poor food') which is very fashionable. There has been a huge upsurge recently in the number of *enoteche* (wine bars) which offer good snacks to go with your wine. Most of these are excellent and provide a less formal yet substantial alternative to a full-blown meal.

At the top end of the scale, fish restaurants are much sought after by the Romans and there are some excellent (albeit expensive) ones to choose between. If you opt for an ordinary restaurant which does not specialise in seafood, you would be well advised to eat in it only on Tuesdays and Fridays when the fish is guaranteed to be fresh.

Most restaurants are stylish and therefore ask you to dress accordingly: in the smartest establishments a jacket (and often tie) is obligatory for men and in many places you will not be admitted in shorts and T-shirts. Style is very important to the Romans and is all part of *la bella figura* – the art of looking and being seen to look your best.

MENUS

Beware of 'tourist menus', they are not usually good value and are of indifferent quality. Occasionally there is no written menu, but do not be fazed by that: take a look at what others are eating and, if it is to your taste, point to it or, at best, try a few words of Italian – your efforts will be much appreciated.

Romans are adapting to less lavish meals, but you will still find the traditional gourmand style of *antipasto* (hors d'oeuvre), followed by *primo* (the all-important pasta course) and *secondo* (usually fish or meat), followed by cheese and/or pudding. Many restaurants have a limited *dolci* selection (with some notable exceptions) and Romans often tend to skip this and opt for a delicious *gelato* (ice cream) and coffee or digestive at a bar later.

MANNERS

If you are ordering house wine, the white Castello Romani variety is usually the safest option. You will often see Romans leaving some wine undrunk in the bottle: this does not mean that it is unpalatable, rather a question of good manners and it is considered very bad form to be drunk. However, smoking is accepted just about everywhere, although it is banned on public transport. Mobile phones are often a fashion accessory in Rome, but their use is becoming increasingly discouraged in smart restaurants.

PAYMENT

Italy is still very much a cash society, so be prepared not to have your credit card accepted everywhere, especially in small eateries. Service is supposed to be included, but an increasing trend nowadays is to add it on separately. However, if the tip is at your discretion then around 10 per cent would be fair for good service. Do try to make sense of the thousands of lire on your bill, especially in touristy areas as it is not unknown for 'extras' to somehow miraculously appear. Also hold on to your receipted bill (*la ricevuta fiscale*) as in theory the 'finance police' can extract a fine running into millions of lire, if you do not have it to hand. (In practice this is mainly aimed at tax-evading restaurateurs.)

CHILDREN

Children are generally made very welcome everywhere, especially at the *pizzerie*. They will love the ice cream parlours for which this city is so renowned and, if all else fails, there are three branches of McDonald's.

OPENING HOURS

Lunch is very important to the Romans so most shops are closed during this sacred time until late afternoon. Many restaurants close in August for the annual holidays (*feragosto*): the shutters come down and, seemingly, all Romans head for the coast. If your favourite restaurant happens to be closed, you owe it to yourself to toss those coins into the Trevi Fountain to ensure your return to this eternally wonderful city!

Menu decoder

MEALS (Pasti)
prima colazione – breakfast
pranzo – lunch
cena – dinner
spuntino – snack
tramezzino – sandwich

COOKING METHODS
affumicato – smoked
al dente – slightly firm (used in pasta dishes)
al forno – cooked in an oven
al vapore – steamed
arrosto – roasted
bollito – boiled
cotto – cooked
crudo – raw
fatto in casa – homemade
forno a legna – cooked in a wood-fired oven
fritto – fried
grigliato – grilled
in bianco – plain, just with butter or oil
in brodo – in clear broth
in umido – poached
ripieno – stuffed
stufato – stewed

BREADS
focaccia – flat, unsalted bread, usually brushed with olive oil and garlic
pane – generic name for bread
panini – bread rolls
pizza a taglio – pizza slice
pizza bianca – plain oiled bread rather like focaccia

APPETISERS (Antipasti)
antipasto di mare – seafood hors d'oeuvre
antipasto misto – a selection of cold meat appetisers with marinated vegetables
bresaola – dry-cured beef
bruschetta – toasted Roman bread rubbed with a clove of garlic and a drizzle of olive oil
carciofi alla romana – globe artichokes stuffed with parsley, anchovies, breadcrumbs and Roman mint
carpaccio – raw sliced lean beef with olive oil, lemon juice and shavings of parmesan cheese
crostini – savoury canapés
fiori di zucchini – fried courgette flowers stuffed with anchovy and mozzarella
mortadella – salami-style salted pork
olive – olives

PRIMI/PIATTI (First course)
agnolotti – pasta similar to ravioli
alla carbonara – sauce with bacon, egg and parmesan cheese
all'amatriciana – sauce of tomato, chilli, onion and sausage
all'arrabbiata – tomato and chilli spicy sauce
alla puttanesca – sauce with olives, garlic and capers in hot oil
alle vongole – Roman clam sauce usually served with spaghetti
al pesto – a sauce of basil, pine nuts and pecorino
al pomodoro – a sauce of fresh, raw tomatoes
al ragù – with tomatoes and minced meat (same as *bolognese*)

brodo – broth
cannelloni – long pasta rolls
fettuccine – long flat pasta strips
gnocchi – dumplings
orecchiette – little ear-shaped
   pasta pieces
pappardelle – a kind of pasta
   similar to wide tagliatelle
tagliatelle – ribbon-like pasta
   often served in cream sauce
taglierini – thin ribbons of pasta
tonnarelli – like large spaghetti
tortellini – pasta whose shape is
   supposedly inspired by
   Venus's navel
zuppa di verdura – vegetable
   soup

FISH AND SEAFOOD
crostacei – shellfish
insalata di mare – seafood salad
fritto misto – mixed fried fish
acciughe – anchovies, also *alici*
aragosta – lobster, also *astice*
baccalà – salted cod
bianchetti – little fish like
   whitebait
calamari – squid
cappe sante – scallops
coda di rospo – monkfish tails
cozze – mussels
gamberetti – shrimps

gamberi – prawns
granchio – crab
merluzzo – cod
ostriche – oysters
pesce – generic word for fish
pesce spada – swordfish
polpo/polipo – octopus
rombo – turbot
rospo – monkfish
San Pietro – John Dory
sarde (sardine) – sardines
spigola – sea bass
sogliola – sole
tonno – tuna
trota salmonata – salmon trout
vongole – clams

MEAT, POULTRY AND GAME
arrosto mista – mixed roast
   meats
caccia – generic term for game
cotoletta – chop
filetto – fillet
abbacchio arrosto – baby roasted
   lamb
agnello – lamb
anatra – duck
animelle – offal
bistecca – beefsteak; *al sangue*,
   rare; *ben cotto*, well done
capretto – kid
cervelle – calves' brains

▲ Fish *antipasto*

cervo – venison
cinghiale – wild boar
coda alla vaccinara – oxtail
    braised in celery broth
coniglio – rabbit
fagiano – pheasant
fegato – liver, usually calves'
maiale – pork
manzo – beef
ossobuco – beef shins containing
    marrow jelly
pajata – veal intestines
pancetta – a thicker kind of
    unsmoked bacon
pollo – chicken
rognoni – kidneys
salsicce – sausages
saltimbocca – veal escalopes
straccetti – strips of veal or beef
    stir-fried
tacchino – turkey
trippa – tripe
vitello – veal

HERBS, PULSES AND VEGETABLES
aglio – garlic
asparagi – asparagus
basilico – basil
broccoletti – tiny broccoli sprigs
capperi – capers
carciofi – leafy globe artichokes
carote – carrots
cavolfiore – cauliflower
ceci – chick peas
cetriolo – cucumber
cipolla – onion
contorni – generic term for
    vegetables
dragoncello – tarragon
fagioli – white beans
fagiolini – green, string or French
    beans
funghi – mushrooms
insalata – salad
lattuga – lettuce
lenticchie – lentils
mandorle – almonds

melanzane – aubergines
menta – mint
patate – potatoes
peperoncino – chilli
peperoni – peppers
pinoli – pine nuts
pinzimonio – selection of raw
    vegetables (crudités) to be
    dipped in olive oil
piselli – peas
pomodoro – tomato
porri – leeks
prezzemolo – parsley
radice – radish
ramerino – rosemary
rucola – rocket salad
sedano – celery
spinaci – spinach
tartufo – truffles
verza – Savoy cabbage
zucchini – courgettes

FRUIT
albicocche – apricots
ananas – pineapple
arance – oranges
banane – bananas
ciliege – cherries
cocomero – watermelon
datteri – dates
fichi – figs
fragole – strawberries
frutti di bosco – woodland berries
lamponi – raspberries
limone – lemons
mele – apples
melone – melons
more – blackberries
pere – pears
pesche – peaches
pompelmo – grapefruit
prugne – plums; also *susine*
uva – grapes

DESSERTS AND CHEESE
amaretti – macaroons
castagnaccio – chestnut cake
cavallucci – spice biscuits with

honey, nuts and candied orange peel

cenci – fritters, with a few drops of marsala or liqueur coated with icing sugar

gelato – ice cream

granità – flavoured ice

mandorlata – almond brittle

montebianco – meringue, cream and *marron glacé purée*

mozzarella – cheese traditionally made from buffalo milk, usually preserved in liquid

pannacotta – 'cooked cream' – a very thick cream often served with a wild berry sauce (*frutti di bosco*) or chocolate

panforte – hard cake made with almonds, honey and dried fruit

panettone – large yeast cake with dried fruit and with a lot of eggs and butter

pecorino – tangy hard cheese made from ewes' milk

ricciarelli – almond biscuits

ricotta – soft white cheese

tiramisù – sponge, mascarpone, coffee and marsala, liberally sprinkled with chocolate

torta della nonna – patisserie cream flan with pine nuts

millefoglie – cake made of flaky pastry (millefeuille)

zabaglione – frothy pudding made with egg yolks, sugar and marsala

DRINKS

acqua (minerale) gassata, senza gas – water (mineral) fizzy, without gas

bicchiere – glass (of wine)

birra – beer; *birra alla spina* (draught beer); sizes are usually *piccola* (small), media (medium) and *grande* (large)

bottiglia – bottle

caffè – coffee; *cappuccino* (coffee with milk froth); *corretto* (with a dash of grappa), *caffè latte* (a milky cappuccino)

cioccolata – hot chocolate

latte – milk

succo di frutta – fruit juice; *una spremuta* – freshly squeezed

tè – tea

vino (rosso, bianco, rosato) – wine (red, white, rosé); dry is *secco*

▲ Sacks of beans and pulses

Recipes

Abbacchio alla cacciatora (huntsman's baby lamb) from Ristorante Checchino dal 1887, Testaccio

Serves 4

INGREDIENTS

1kg of tender leg of lamb deboned

2 salted anchovies

2 red chillies

1 clove of garlic

salt and pepper to taste

½ glass of dry white wine from the Castelli Romani region

½ glass of wine vinegar

3–4 tablespoons of extra virgin olive oil

Cut the lamb into small pieces. In a cast-iron or non-stick pan, fry the two anchovies, deboned and desalted, in the olive oil, stirring all the time. Add the clove of garlic and continue to stir, making sure that the ingredients do not brown too quickly.

As soon as the garlic is lightly coloured add the lamb and the red chillies cut into pieces. (If you are using fresh chillies slice them under running water to avoid burning your fingers and remove the seeds if you like a less hot flavour.) Brown all the ingredients, stirring constantly over a brisk flame. Season to taste with sea salt and freshly milled black pepper. Once the lamb pieces are brown, add the wine and vinegar and check the seasoning again. Cover the pan, lower the heat and leave to cook until tender. Serve hot.

Spigola alla romana (sea bass with mushrooms, Roman style)

Serves 4

INGREDIENTS

1kg fillets of sea bass

200g fresh mushrooms (or dried *porcini*, soaked beforehand in water)

3 chopped shallots

1 clove garlic

2 anchovy fillets in oil

4 tablespoons white Castelli Romani wine

20g butter (unsalted)

4 tablespoons extra virgin olive oil

1 tablespoon plain flour

1 tablespoon chopped parsley (reserving a few whole leaves for decoration)

freshly ground salt and pepper

Rub the sea bass fillets with salt and pepper. Brown the shallots with the garlic in the butter and oil, add the chopped anchovy fillets and cook them until they dissolve, mashing them with a fork. Add the sea bass fillets, sprinkle them with the wine and cook quickly on each side. Drain carefully and keep warm.

Toss the mushrooms in the flour and add them to the pan. Taste for salt, add pepper and then cook over a lively flame for five to six minutes. Remove the pan from the flame, add the parsley and pour the sauce over the fillets, which should still be warm. Garnish with whole parsley leaves.

Spaghetti alla carbonara (spaghetti with egg and guanciale or pancetta)

Serves 4

INGREDIENTS

400g spaghetti

100g *guanciale* (unsmoked bacon from the hog's jowl instead of the belly) or very lean *pancetta* (unsmoked bacon)

1 tablespoon extra virgin olive oil

30g butter

3 eggs

40g each pecorino (ewes' cheese) and parmesan cheese freshly grated together

salt and freshly ground pepper

Bring a large pan of salted water to the boil and cook the pasta *al dente*. (Fresh pasta takes roughly half the time of the packeted variety). Meanwhile, fry the diced *guanciale* (*pancetta*) in a small pan with the oil.

Beat the eggs in a bowl with half the cheese, salt and pepper. Heat the butter in a saucepan until it is nutty brown, pour in the eggs and mix very quickly. Add the drained pasta, *guanciale* or *pancetta* and the rest of the cheese.

Remove from the heat and stir the pasta in the pan for a few seconds and serve. The result should be smooth and creamy. (You can cheat by adding a tablespoon of cream to the egg mixture, but it's not the authentic Roman way!)

Carciofi alla giudia
(fried whole artichokes from the ghetto)

INGREDIENTS

Roman artichokes – the large globe variety characteristic of the Lazio region (not to be confused with the knobbly 'Jerusalem' artichoke)

extra virgin olive oil

lemon

salt and pepper

Remove the tough outer leaves of the artichokes and cut off their stems. Cut off the tips of the leaves with a very sharp knife, then drop the artichokes immediately into cold water with lemon juice, drain and let dry.

Press the artichokes delicately, head down on the work surface, so that the leaves open up like a flower.

Heat a generous amount of oil in a large pan and drop the artichokes in head first, keeping them pressed on the bottom with a fork until they are nicely browned. Turn them over and cook until the heart is tender.

Drain well on paper towels and season with salt and pepper just before serving.

Timballo di ricotta
(timbale of ricotta)

Serves 4 (generously)

INGREDIENTS

700g sheeps' milk ricotta

230g confectioners' sugar

½ unwaxed lemon

¼ cup brandy

5 eggs

pinch ground cinnamon

Beat the egg yolks with the sugar with an electric beater. When smooth and pale, add the ricotta, grated rind of the lemon, cinnamon and brandy. Beat the egg whites until stiff and fold them delicately into the ricotta mixture. Pour into a well-greased flan mould and bake in a preheated oven at about 180°C for about 20 minutes. Lower the temperature to 150°C and continue baking for another 10 minutes.

▲ *Carciofi*

Published by Thomas Cook Publishing
Thomas Cook Holdings Ltd
PO Box 227
Thorpe Wood
Peterborough PE3 6PU
United Kingdom

Telephone: 01733 503571
Email: books@thomascook.com

Text © 2001 Thomas Cook Publishing
Maps © 2001 Thomas Cook Publishing

ISBN 1 841570 60 5

Distributed in the United States of
America by the Globe Pequot Press,
PO Box 480, Guilford, Connecticut
06437, USA

Publisher: Donald Greig
Commissioning Editor: Deborah Parker
Map Editor: Bernard Horton

Project management: Dial House
    Publishing
Series Editor: Christopher Catling
Copy Editor: Lucy Thomson
Proofreader: Jan Wiltshire

Series and cover design: WhiteLight
Cover artwork: WhiteLight and
    Kaarin Wall
Text layout: SJM Design Consultancy,
    Dial House Publishing
Maps prepared by Polly Senior
    Cartography

Repro and image setting: PDQ Digital
    Media Solutions Ltd
Printed and bound in Italy by
    Eurografica SpA

Written and researched by **Adele Evans**

The author would like to thank Christine
Braganza for her invaluable support (and
translation help with the recipes).

We would like to thank the author for the
photographs used in this book, to whom
the copyright belongs, with the exception
of the following:
Checchino dal 1887 (page 11)
John Heseltine (pages 39, 50, 60, 61, 65,
    73, 79, 81 and 82)
Caroline Jones (page 3)
Neil Setchfield (pages 13 and 87)
Starwood Hotels (pages 46, 47 and 56).

The contents of this book are believed to
be correct at the time of printing.
Establishments may open, close or change
and Thomas Cook Holdings Ltd cannot
accept responsibility for errors or
omissions, or for the consequences of any
reliance on the information provided.
Descriptions and assessments are given in
good faith but are based on the authors'
views and experience at the time of
writing and therefore contain an element
of subjective opinion which may not
accord with the reader's subsequent
experiences. The opinions in this book do
not necessarily represent those of
Thomas Cook Holdings Ltd.